JUJITSU
NERVE TECHNIQUES
The Invisible Weapon of Self-Defense

by George Kirby

JUJITSU NERVE TECHNIQUES
The Invisible Weapon of Self-Defense

by George Kirby

Edited by Raymond Horwitz and Janina Wilson

Graphic design by John Bodine

Third printing 2004

ISBN 0-89750-412-X

WARNING

BLACK BELT BOOKS
A Division of **OHARA ⑪ PUBLICATIONS, INC.**
World Leader in Martial Arts Publications

ACKNOWLEDGMENTS

Whenever I conduct a seminar, I consider it successful only if I too have learned something. It may be a new technique, a variation of a move or an exchange of ideas. Unless I keep an open mind and am willing to learn, there is no growth; my mind and body cannot prosper. It is much like taking a pathway up a mountain. There may be more than one way, but each has its own characteristics that need to be explored, studied and reflected upon.

The same concept applies to writing a book such as this. When I started writing, I had a certain level of knowledge and understanding. By the time I finished, both had grown tremendously as a result of the generosity of a number of people who walked with me on one of the paths up the mountainside:

- Rhonda Hyatt, athletic director at California State University Northridge (CSUN), and Nadine Steg, certified physical therapist assistant and licensed massage therapist, both of whom assisted in the cross-referencing of nerves, pressure points, trigger points and muscle groups. Many thanks to Sensei Marty Noel of the Northeast Martial Arts Institute for introducing me to Nadine.

- Sensei Mark Jordan, Ron Sekulich, Michael Sebastian and Anthony Damigo, who really discovered the use of nerve and pressure points while serving as training partners for this book.

- Professors Sanzo Seki (Jack M. Haywood deceased), Nicholas Kring (deceased) and Kenneth Penland, whose unselfish teaching and guidance provided me with the knowledge and understanding of *shioku waza* (pain and/or nerve techniques).

From left to right: Michael Sebastian (shodan), Mark Jordan (sandan),
Professor George Kirby (judan), Ron Sekulich (sandan) and Anthony Damigo (nidan).

DEDICATION

I dedicate this book to the two most important people in my life: my wife, Adel, and my daughter Kimberly. I would like to thank Adel for her tremendous patience as I spent the many hours necessary to compile and write this book. I would also like to thank Kimberly, who has made it a habit to choose the most inopportune times to surreptitiously entrap me in various *jujitsu* holds, locks and nerve techniques she has learned during the first 15 years of her life, thus reassuring me that the art does work and the pain is real. I love you both. Thank you.

—George Kirby

ABOUT THE AUTHOR

In 1968, George Kirby had no idea where martial arts training would take him. He was a first-degree brown belt (*ikkyu*) in Sensei Jack "Sanzo" Seki's jujistu program at Los Angeles Valley College. It was a class he took purely for relaxation from the stress of studying for his Master of Arts degree exams at California State University, Los Angeles.

A twist of fate landed Kirby in a very interesting predicament when Seki went up to Kirby and said, "Georgie, I want you and Bill Fromm (another brown belt) to take over the Burbank YMCA program. The instructor has to leave."

Kirby responded, "Sensei, I'm only a brown belt. How can I teach a class?"

"Bill knows more techniques, but you're a [school] teacher, so you can both teach the class."

Kirby continued his protest: "But sensei, we're only brown belts."

Seki put an end to the debate by declaring, "Now you're both black belts. Act like it."

And thus Kirby's life as a *sensei* (teacher) began. Sensei Seki, according to Kirby, never asked his students to do something. He simply told them. Years later, Seki would tell Kirby he had faith in his abilities to perform well as a sensei. It appears that Seki was correct—Kirby has been a sensei for 34 years.

Kirby took on his position at the Burbank YMCA in 1968. The program moved to the City of Burbank Parks and Recreation Department in 1974, where it continues to this day. That year, he met his future wife, Adel, who is also a school teacher. They married in 1976 and were blessed in 1986 with their daughter, Kimberly, who Kirby says, "is growing up to be a caring and well-educated young lady."

Kirby left the Burbank Parks program in 1996 to start a new jujitsu ("gentle art") program with the City of Santa Clarita Parks and Recreation Department, where he still teaches classes on a weekly basis. During the late 1970s to 1983, Kirby taught social studies and jujitsu (as an elective class or for physical education credit) at Olive Vista Junior High School in Sylmar, California. His jujitsu class was overwhelmingly popular, growing to four classes out of his five-period day by the time he left the school in January 1983.

Among Kirby's most lasting contributions to the martial arts has been the American Ju-Jitsu Association (AJA), which he formed with Bill Fromm at the suggestion of Seki. By the late 1970s, the AJA had become the national governing body of jujitsu and, under IRS code 501c3, established itself as an amateur athletic association. The organization has continued to grow in size and influence over the years, handling a number of *ryu* (styles) of jujitsu and becoming an internationally-recognized governing body. Although he initially served as president of the AJA, the administrative duties of the organization have been delegated to others in recent years. Kirby now serves as chairman of its board of directors. In addition, he is also the founder and chairman of the board of directors of the Budoshin Ju-Jitsu Dojo, Inc., a non-profit educational foundation, and the Budoshin Ju-Jitsu Yudanshakai, a research and educational foundation.

In 1994, Kirby was one of several nationally recognized martial artists to be selected by the Los Angeles Police Department (LAPD) to develop a new arrest-and-control program following the Rodney King controversy. That core of marital artists became known as the Civilian Martial Arts Advisory Panel (CMAAP). As a defensive tactics consultant for the LAPD, Kirby continued to serve law enforcement through the CMAAP, dealing with issues involving officer safety in the areas of arrest and control. During that time, he met top martial artists from other arts, working with them for a common purpose. In 1998, the City of Los Angeles awarded all the CMAAP members Certificates of Appreciation for their commitment to developing one of the nation's top arrest-and-control training programs.

Amidst the flurry of all his prestigious public work, writing had always been a dream of this martial arts expert. Although several of his articles had been published in *Black Belt* in the late 1970s and early 1980s, writing a book on jujitsu had been somewhat of a remote fantasy for Kirby. However, all that changed in 1982 at the Ohara Publications/Black Belt Communications office. Kirby was conversing with Gregory Lee, a former Ohara/Black Belt editor, when he ran into then-Assistant Publisher Geri Simon. Lee introduced the two of them, at which point Simon mentioned she was considering a book on jujitsu and asked if Kirby was interested in submitting a proposal. Of course, he was and did—and the rest is history.

Since that day of opportunity, Kirby has written three books before this one for Black Belt Communications: *Jujitsu: Basic Techniques of the Gentle Art* (1983), *Jujitsu: Intermediate Techniques of the Gentle Art* (1985) and *Jutte: Power of Ten Hands Weapon* (1987). He has also self-published *Budoshin Ju-Jitsu: The Big Book*, which is now in its fifth edition. Kirby has also produced an eight-tape video series titled *Budoshin Ju-Jitsu Black Belt Home Study Course* for Panther Productions. The videos correlate with the concepts presented in his books, creating what Kirby calls "a tremendously useful instructional resource for the serious martial artist."

Kirby has also been involved with a number of national and international organizations. He is currently a member of the World Grandmaster Council, Dai Nippon Seibukan Budo/Bugei-kai (All-Japan Martial Arts and Ways Association), the World Martial Arts Accreditation Council, International Jujitsu Federation Nippon Seibukan, and the American Society for Law Enforcement Training, among others.

In 1997, Kirby received the title of *hanshi* (master). And in 2000, he was promoted to *judan* (10th-*dan* black belt) in jujitsu. This distinguished career in the martial arts began as an effort to relax during intensive master's degree studies (which paid off when Kirby received his Master's in Social Science in 1969). It has led to a career as a jujitsu instructor, martial arts council member, and published author in addition to his academic career. Since 1995, he has been the Social Science Department Chairperson at Ulysses S. Grant High School in Van Nuys, California, where he teaches Honors Economics, Honors Government and Advanced Placement Government.

In connecting his academic and martial arts careers, Kirby says, "Teaching jujitsu and social sciences in public school is still fun and enjoyable because the students and the intrinsic rewards of teaching have made it so. It is an honor to be a teacher, a sensei."

INTRODUCTION

This book is unique to the martial arts community because it opens up the area of shioku waza to all martial arts styles and practitioners. It will make it possible for you, regardless of your proficiency, rank or level of knowledge, to add the important element of shioku waza to your repertoire and become a more proficient and responsible martial artist.

The working knowledge you gain from the following pages may help you learn techniques that are secret in many ryu. Some of the nerve points themselves may be considered secret by some ryu and taught only to higher-ranking students because they have the technical expertise and maturity to use them effectively and responsibly.

Gained knowledge means added responsibility. Utilizing nerve techniques allows you to employ much less force to control your attacker, significantly reducing the level of violence involved in martial arts maneuvers. This also allows you to act more responsibly simply because less force is needed to protect yourself.

This book is an exceptional resource, for it contains more information on the use of nerve techniques than any previously published marital arts book. It cross-references nerve and pressure points, meridian points, trigger points, nerves and muscle groups with each other as well as effective street self-defense techniques. It also provides information on *atemi waza* (attacking vital areas), *ki* (energy flow) and *mushin* (empty/clear mind) in the context of training to increase the effectiveness of nerve techniques. Furthermore, this text provides realistic training procedures based on my more than 30 years of experience in teaching the art of jujitsu.

The material contained in this book may also change your art. If you are a sensei, it may change the way you teach. Of course, this raises the issue of conflict between tradition and change. How do you deal with this issue? Will adding the knowledge in this book change your ryu? How will you deal with this change? The chapter entitled "Change: Foundations, Traditions and Pedestals" will deal with these and other topics, hopefully providing a sound philosophical platform from which to proceed as you see fit.

The techniques contained in this book will help you become a more effective and well-rounded martial artist, reducing the amount of force required to protect yourself by replacing a formerly devastating blow with a slight touch. You will have quick, subtle and effective control over your attacker—all with minimal use of your ki for maximum benefit.

TABLE OF CONTENTS

CHAPTER 1
Atemi Waza: Secret Behind the Art of Jujitsu 13

CHAPTER 2
Ki, Mushin and Self-Defense 27

CHAPTER 3
Pain and Compliance 41

CHAPTER 4
Ow! Relieving the Angst of Pressure-Point Training 47

CHAPTER 5
Change: Foundations, Traditions and Pedestals.......................... 55

CHAPTER 6
Bringing It All Together 65

CHAPTER 7
Pressure-Point Techniques 69

CHAPTER 8
Balance Points... 219

CHAPTER 9
Balance-Point Techniques 225

GLOSSARY 235

RECOMMENDED READING 237

CHAPTER 1

ATEMI WAZA:
SECRET BEHIND THE ART
OF JUJITSU

Jujitsu is referred to as the gentle art of self-defense because it requires very little effort on the part of the defender; the attacker does most, if not all, of the work.[1] You, the defender, simply control the attacker's ki.

On the one hand, it really is a gentle art, allowing a person who's proficient in its practice to control his opponent with minimal pain or discomfort. Furthermore, once this skill is mastered, you can effectively utilize your self-defense knowledge and maneuvers at any level of intensity, using your attacker's ki as the basis for your techniques. If necessary, you can deliver devastating maneuvers that will leave your assailant disabled on the ground and completely unable to continue the attack.

There are many skills that make such a broad-spectrum approach to self-defense possible. One of the major skills essential to perfecting the art of jujitsu is a thorough working knowledge of atemi waza, otherwise known as attacking vital areas of the body. Atemi waza is not a secret set of techniques taught only at advanced levels of a specific martial art. In fact, it is used in all martial arts to some extent. Atemi waza is so important to jujitsu because it makes it possible for you to become more effective in all the other aspects of the art: *judo* (throws and pins), *aikido* (joint locks and using attacker's ki or momentum) and *karatedo* (hits and kicks). Most importantly, atemi waza allows you to establish control over your attacker, which makes all other techniques easier to execute.

Characteristics of Atemi Waza

First, you need to clear your mind of any preconceived notions regarding atemi waza. It is not solely limited to "death touches" or "death blows." Those are misnomers created to justify the illusion that atemi waza is so devastating that it's to be used only in life-and-death situations and therefore taught only to qualified upper belts who have the skill and judgment to use atemi waza properly. At the other extreme, atemi waza is not just a set of subtle, quicker-than-the-eye moves performed by some old martial arts master that leaves his assailant crumbling to the ground in an unconscious or incapacitated state. Atemi waza is these two extremes and everything between, including light touches in vital areas for distraction purposes as well as devastating blows that can seriously or fatally injure an attacker if used carelessly. Perhaps it might be best if the concept of atemi waza were deconstructed so as to remove some of the mystique surrounding it.

---

1. *ju* = gentle, *jistu* = art

PRESSURE-POINT REFERENCE TABLE

No.	Description	Nerve(s)	Effect	Trigger Pt./Muscle Group.	Merid. Pt.
1	center of forehead	facial	M	frontalis	GB-14
2	ridge above eyes	supraorbital	LM	frontalis	B-2
3	eyes		S		
4	temple	zygomaticotemporalis	MS	temporalis	TW-23 GB-1
5	ridge at base of eyes	infraorbital	MS		ST-1
6	side base of nose (next to nostril)	infraorbital	LM		LI-20
7	ears (insert finger)		M		
8	side of jaw (in a line from base of nose to mid-ear)	zygomatic branch facial	MS	masseter	GB-3
9	cheekbone (below eyes)	infraorbital (facial buccal branch)	MS	zygomaticus major	ST-2
10	tip of nose	external nasal	MS		GV-25
11	philtrum (base of nose)	infraorbital (sup. labial)	MS		GV-26
12	under chin	mertalis	LM		
13	Whitney's Notch (rear center base of skull)	accessory	MS	trapezius	GV-16
14	base of skull (rear, 1 to 2 inches right of center)	occipital	S	trapezius	B-10
15	mastoid nerve (under ear)	auricular, hypoglossal, vagus	LM	sternocleidomastoid (sternal head)	TW-17
16	just behind lower part of jawbone	vagus (trigeminal)	LMS	posterior digastric	SI-17
17	under jaw	auricular, hypoglossal, vagus (mylohyoid)	LMS	anterior digastric	SI-17 LI-18
18	side of neck, halfway down, front of sternocleidomastoid muscle	supraclavicular	LMS		LI-17
19	base of neck, directly down from mastoid (clavical notch)	supraclavicular (spinal accessory)	LM	upper trapezius	LI-17 ST-12

No.	Description	Nerve(s)	Effect	Trigger Pt./Muscle Group.	Merid. Pt.
20	larynx	vagus, cervical, cardiac	MS		S-9 S-10
21	base of neck (at artery toward front of neck)	phrenic (auricular)	LMS	sternocleidomastoid (sternal head)	ST-11
22	jugular (suprasternal) notch	supraclavicular	MS		CV-22
23	center of neck (rear) at second cervical vertebra	accessory	MS	trapezius	
24	base of neck (rear)		MS	cervical seven vertebra	GV-14
25	rear side base of skull, between trapezius and sternocleidomastoid muscle	accessory (occipital [dorsal rami mid-lower cervical nerves])	MS	trapezius (splenius captis)	GB-20
26	one-third of the way down from neck at collarbone	brachial plexus (auricular plus others)	MS		TW-15 ST-12
27	top and front of shoulder joint	supraclavicular (median, ulnar, radial and axillary)	LMS	brachial plexus (complex of nerves: med., rad., uln.)	LI-16
28	front of shoulder at 2 o'clock	axillary (medial pectoral)	LM	pectoralis minor	LU-1
29	just inside front of shoulder joint	axillary (brachial plexus)	LMS	anterior deltoid	LU-2
30	armpit, upward and inward toward head	brachial plexus (nerve group: med./rad./uln./ med. cutaneous)	LM		H-1
31	just below LU-1 (point 28: front of shoulder at 2 o'clock)	lateral pectoral (mediaband lateral pectoral)	LMS	pectoralis major	ST-13
32	front of chest at intersection of horizontal line at armpit and vertical line running down from side of neck	medial and lateral pectoral	BP	pectoralis major	K-24
33	sternum (level with nipples)	intercostal	LMS		CV-17
34	zyphoid process		S		CV-16
35	solar plexus		MS		CV-15
36	side base of ribs (floating ribs)	intercostal	MS		GB-25 LV-13

No.	Description	Nerve(s)	Effect	Trigger Pt./Muscle Group.	Merid. Pt.
37	hypogastrum (about 1 inch below navel)	iliohypogastric	MS		CV-6
38	front of stomach, midway between front and side	anterior cutaneous	LM		ST-25 K-16
39	four inches below navel (*saiki tanden*)		MS (BP)		CV-4
40	bladder	intercostal nerves (T7-12)	MS	rectus abdominis	CV-2 CV-3
41	femoral artery pressure point (just outside)	femoral	LM		SP-12
42	groin		MS		CV-1
43	center of crotch	prostate	S		
44	front side of hip	lateral cutaneous	LMS	tensor fascae latae	GB-28
45	shoulder top, halfway between neck and shoulder joint	cranial XII (spinal accessory, supraclavicular)	LM	upper trapezius	GB-21
46	rear of shoulder, halfway between neck and shoulder joint	cranial XII (spinal accessory, lateral)	LM	upper trapezius	TW-15
47	rear of shoulder (superior scapula)	suprascapular, musculocutaneous	LM	levator scapula	B-14 B-36
48	trapezius (between vertebrae and shoulder blades)	dorsal scapular	MS	rhomboids (lower)	B-39
49	trapezius muscle, lower	dorsal rami of spinal nerves	M	splenius cervicis	B-38
50	kidneys	thoracic (intercostal nerves T12-L2)	MS	lower quadratus lumborum	B-47
51	side, below ribs, slightly to back side	lateral cutaneous	LM	quadratus/external oblique	GB-25
52	center base at tailbone (coccyx)	sciatic	BP		GV-1 B-31 to B-34
53	rear side of hip	superior gluteal	LMS	gluteus minimus	GB-28 GB-29

No.	Description	Nerve(s)	Effect	Trigger Pt./Muscle Group.	Merid. Pt.
54	rear of hip, lower back	sciatic (sacral nerves, first and second)	BP	piriformis	
55	crotch, rectum (anus/sphincter muscle)	sphincter	MS		
56	nail, under thumb and fingers 1, 2 and 3 (inside)	median	LM		
57	nail, under fingers 3 and 4 (outside)	ulnar	LM		
58	between thumb and finger 1	radial	L	first dorsal interosseus	LI-4
59	back of hand, between fingers 1 and 2	radial	LM	second dorsal interosseus	P-8
60	back of hand, between fingers 2 and 3 (inside)	digital	LM	second dorsal interosseus	
61	back of hand, between fingers 3 and 4	ulnar	LM	dorsal interosseus	TW-3 H-8
62	base of little finger, below knuckle	ulnar	LM	(boney)	SI-3
63	wrist (at base of ulnar)	ulnar	L	flexor carpi ulnaris	LU-9
64	wrist (inside base) between radius and ulnar bones	median	LM	flexor pollicus longus	P-7
65	wrist joint (little finger side)	ulnar	LMS	abductor minimi	LI-5 LU-5
66	wrist joint (thumb side)	radial	LMS	extensor pollicus longus	SI-5 SI-6 H-7
67	forearm (halfway down at base of brachoradialis)	cutaneous, radial	LM	brachoradialis (base)	LU-6
68	one-third of the way down inside forearm	ulnar	LMS	flexor digitorum superficialis (humeral head)	LU-6
69	one-quarter of the way down inside top of forearm	radial	LM	supinator	LU-6
70	outside back of elbow, about one-third of the way down	radial, musculocutaneous	LM	extensor carpi radialis longus	LI-10

No.	Description	Nerve(s)	Effect	Trigger Pt./Muscle Group.	Merid. Pt.
71	middle of elbow, front crease	median	LM	biceps tendon	P-3 LU-5
72	above elbow on tricep tendon	radial	LM	triceps brachii (medial head)	H-3 HC-3
73	inside of elbow at base of bicep tendon	radial, median	LM	pronator teres	P-3
74	inside of elbow just above elbow joint	median, musculocutaneous	LM	brachialis	L-5
75	inside of elbow halfway down from shoulder below bicep	ulnar, median	LM	triceps brachii	H-2
76	back of elbow (inside)	ulnar (inside)	MS	triceps brachii (medial head)	SI-8
77	back of elbow (outside)	radial (outside)	MS	extensor carpi radialis	LI-11
78	back of elbow (center)	radial	MS	triceps brachii (medial head)	TW-10 TW-11
79	upper arm (outside, back, tricep, halfway down)	radial	LM	triceps brachii	TW-12
80	brachioradialis muscle (base and halfway down upper arm [biceps])	musculocutaneous	M	biceps	L-4
81	big toe	deep peroneal (medial plantar)	LM	extensor hallicus	SP-1 LV-1
82	toes	deep peroneal	LM	extensor digitorum	GB-44 B-67 ST-44 ST-45
83	valley between large and second toes	deep peroneal	LMS	dorsal interosseous	LV-2
84	instep	deep peroneal (dorsal digital, lateral and medial plantar)	MS	extensor digitorum	ST-43 GB-41 LV-3
85	front of foot and ankle joint (instep)	deep peroneal	LMS	tibialis anterior	ST-41 GB-40
86	just above anklebone on inside of foot	tibial	LMS	tibialis posterior	KI-6 KI-7

No.	Description	Nerve(s)	Effect	Trigger Pt./Muscle Group.	Merid. Pt.
87	just above the outside anklebone on outside of foot	superficial peroneal	M	peroneus	BL-59 BL-60
88	heel at Achilles tendon	tibial	MS	Achilles tendon (gastroc/soleus)	K-3
89	base of calf muscle	tibial	LMS	soleus	B-57
90	one-third of the way down the shin	deep peroneal (princeps pollicus and radialis)	LM	anterior tibialis	ST-38 ST-39
91	behind knee joint, just below knee	tibial, saphenous	LMS	gastrocnemius (nerve: tibialis posterior)	B-54
92	outer side of knee joint, just below knee	peroneal, superficial	LMS	peroneus longus	GB-33 GB-34
93	front of kneecap	saphenous branches	MS	vastus medialus	ST-35
94	outside rear of knee joint	sciatic	LMS	biceps femoris	B-53
95	center of knee joint	popliteal (tibial)	LM	popliteal (nerve: gastrocnemius)	B-54
96	back side of thigh, two-thirds of the way down	sciatic	LMS	biceps femoris	GB-32
97	outside front side of thigh, three-quarters of the way down	femoral (lateral cutaneous)	LMS	vastus lateralis	ST-34
98	about 3 inches above knee joint on outside	sciatic (femoral cutaneous)	LMS	biceps femoris	ST-34
99	inside thigh, midway between kneecap and hip joint	internal cutaneous (obturator and saphenous [the latter coming from femoral nerve])	L	abductor magnus and gracilis	SP-11
100	inside thigh, about one-quarter of the way down from crotch	internal cutaneous (obturator)	LM	abductor longus/bevis	LV-10

Conclusions

Atemi waza is an essential element within your arsenal of self-defense techniques that can be taught to you at any level of proficiency and applied to any martial art. Proper implementation can bring an attacker under your control with a minimal use of force.

While useful for setting up an attacker for shioku waza, atemi waza will not be effective unless you, the defender, can maintain your ki and kuzushi, as well as work from a state of mushin. These three elements are essential for a succesful defense. In the next chapter, we will explore the interrelationship of ki, kuzushi and mushin so you can use shioku waza to your maximum benefit.

As a martial artist, you are also expected to use your knowledge in a responsible manner, responding with what the courts consider reasonable force. Ideally, you shouldn't have to worry about an attacker's well-being in the course of defending yourself. However, this is not so simple in the modern world. As I am neither an attorney nor a judge, I will not attempt to define what reasonable force means outside of using good judgment when defending yourself. If a person grabs your shirt, it may be reasonable to execute a release from his grip and, if necessary, place him into some type of control hold. You would not be justified in striking his face, breaking his nose and jumping on him once he is down. The former might be considered an example of reasonable force. The latter would be an example of excessive force, which might end up putting you behind bars and/or at the losing end of a lawsuit.

As you can see, when developing the ability to defend yourself from a state of mushin, you must also have the awareness to use sufficient force in protecting yourself without going overboard. This makes the task infinitely more difficult. However, this is a reality which must be considered in today's world. Acting responsibly is expected to be part of martial artists' training.

How do you develop this ability? Through practice! You must study in an instructional program where you are trained to not think and yet react automatically in a responsible and reasonable manner. If you have developed your techniques to the point where they are automatic reactions, then you can start to deal with self-defense situations in a more realistic manner. You can alter your responses through practice, depending on the given situation. Your mind will automatically react differently if you are confronted by one person who has merely grabbed your arm as compared to multiple attackers or a person with a weapon. Different responses are required for different situations and must be automatic if you are going to survive. They will be automatic only if you can put yourself into a state of mushin where you are sufficiently relaxed and your mind and body can operate at their full potential.

The specific types of practice that will help you execute shioku waza from a state of mushin can be broken down into three areas:

- *kata* (specific form or technique) practice,

- attack/defense practice, and

- ki development.

Practice in these three areas can initially be done separately. However, eventually they must be integrated if the practice is to be of any long-term value. In fact, this integration should begin as soon as possible. You do not have to be proficient in kata before dealing with self-defense situations or ki development. All three can be worked on simultaneously. Growth will be evident as you continue to study your martial art and improve your proficiency in using shioku waza.

Kata Practice

Kata practice is of absolute importance because it helps you learn how to execute shioku waza correctly from a balanced position. It helps you learn where your body must be at different stages of the technique and how it should feel.[2] In jujitsu, you will also develop a feel for the body of your uke—ranging from no resistance to moderately strong resistance to your techniques. If you are executing a technique correctly, you will know where his body will be as well as where it is going.

In jujitsu, your repertoire will eventually be based on your knowledge and the particular abilities of your body. (This, by the way, is one of the advantages of jujitsu. The art can be adjusted to your abilities; no two black belts will have the same "personal" repertoire.) Continual practice in this area will help you execute specific techniques without any conscious thinking. Eventually, you will also integrate situation-specific techniques to handle a wide variety of potential encounter scenarios.

Attack/Defense Practice

Attack/defense practice is essential to developing your response to unanticipated aggression. Initially, you should know how your uke will attack you. This helps establish certain patterns within your brain. To train in this area of jujitsu, you can try a variety of activities.

First, start by using the same technique for the same attack until you become proficient in its execution. Then add techniques to counter each attack until you have a few techniques for each type of situation. The third step is to have your uke use different attacks while you defend yourself with the same technique for each encounter. This can eventually

---

2. In jujitsu, a technique may refer to a specific kata, such as a *koshi nage* (hip throw) or a *waza* (complete technique) that includes a release or block, a follow-through throw, takedown (or control hold) and a submission which may be executed in the form of a pin, choke, strike, hit, kick or a control hold. See *Jujitsu: Basic Techniques of the Gentle Art* and *Jujitsu: Intermediate Techniques of the Gentle Art* for additional details on kata and waza in jujitsu.

be expanded to several types of attacks and defensive techniques executed in a specific order.

The last stage in the basic development would be for your uke to attack any way he wishes and for you to execute any techniques that come to mind. You may have to proceed slowly, especially when encountering an attack you haven't dealt with before. However, this is the point of the training—to help you realize techniques you know can be used in unexpected situations.

This method of practice should be performed for a specific time period, such as five to 10 attacks each before switching attack/defense roles. Also, have your partner continuously attack you with street-type maneuvers for one minute and then switch so you attack him. As you develop proficiency in your knowledge of kata, your movements will become smoother and your speed will also increase as more of your actions become automatic. Eventually, attacks can be completely random, but your mind and body will react automatically.

The street-attack format is the most effective way to determine your state of mushin. It involves being attacked for one minute and bringing your opponent down or under control each time. Then you allow him to get up and attack again, repeating this process as many times as possible within one minute. After that minute is up, if you have no idea what techniques you did, feel fairly exhilarated (but not tired), and a qualified observer tells you that your execution of techniques was good, you have achieved a state of mushin. In this condition, your ki will flow, allowing you to execute shioku waza effortlessly and flawlessly. As you progress through these stages, you should also be working on reducing your reaction time to any attack. Again, this can be accomplished through practice.

Dojo Practice

The ideal way to execute such practice is in a *dojo* (training hall) where the sensei will have his students line up in two teams, each facing a partner. The sensei will stand on one side of the lineup so one row of students can see him; the others will have their backs to him. The sensei will then order an attack. Initially, the sensei may use a verbal command to signal the uke to attack the *tori* (person executing the technique). Eventually, as the students become more skilled, a visual signal can replace the verbal one. This helps the defending students concentrate on their attackers rather than waiting for a sound from the sensei to announce the start of the exercise. Students can then trade off with each other so that both partners practice this kata.

Regardless of the student's technical proficiency, this exercise can be carried one step further: To demonstrate the attack for the uke to use, visually signal the uke to attack the tori. Then stop the tori's action almost immediately after body contact has been made or the tori commences his response. In this exercise, it is not necessary to allow the tori to complete the technique. If the body of the tori is moving, his mind has probably already decided which technique will be executed next. Since the sequence has been established, there is no need to follow through with the actual technique for post-exchange analysis.

There are a variety of other exercises that can help develop the attack/defense skill. All of these ideally require a dojo situation where there is close supervision by the sensei. One exercise is called the Circle of Fear. In this exercise, all the students face each other in a circle, spaced about 3 feet apart. One student is selected to walk around the circle from the outside while a second student walks in the opposite direction inside the circle. At the sensei's verbal or visual signal, the two walking students (uke) attack the nearest student (tori) standing in the circle. The tori then executes whatever technique automatically comes to mind. In this exercise, it is possible for a tori to be attacked from the front, rear or both directions at the same time. Once an attack has started, the students who have not been attacked should step out of the circle to give the attacked students room to maneuver and execute their techniques.

A second, more intense exercise is called the Triangle. Only four students (of similar proficiency) are needed for this exercise, but it requires much closer supervision than the Circle of Fear. In this exercise, one student (tori) is in the center with three other students (uke) surrounding him. The uke are numbered 1, 2 and 3. The sensei may use verbal or visual signals to indicate which uke is to attack the tori. They may attack in any way they wish, including the use of weapons. However, the use of rubber or wood knives, plastic or rubber clubs (a golf club tube cut in half with the metal ring cut off makes an excellent club), and an *obi* (belt) is strongly recommended over the use of real weapons in all defense training. This allows the uke to attack with moderate or full force as deemed appropriate.

Although this exercise is usually begun quite slowly to allow the tori to execute complete techniques, it is quickly sped up to the point where the tori can no longer respond adequately to the unrelenting attacks of the uke. This exercise works very well with intermediate and advanced students (*yonkyu* [four degrees below black belt] and higher). It forces them to react automatically to situations because there isn't time to think.

In practicing these exercises, there are a few important things to keep in mind:

- A sensei must supervise the activity closely.

- Attacks should not be executed at full force. Students must be aware that these exercises are designed to improve certain essential skills, not to see if an attack can be completed before the tori can execute a response.

- The tori must develop self-control in the execution of techniques, realizing that the uke are restraining themselves. This is a learning experience, not a street situation.

All of these exercises will help the student develop his ability to respond to attacks. They are designed to help the student not to think, but to react to the attack and effectively protect themselves within the framework and philosophy of jujitsu and shioku waza.

Ki Development

Ki development is an essential element in attaining proficiency in any martial art, especially shioku waza. Since you can't see or hear ki, it is essential that you develop the ability to sense and use an attacker's ki. There are two simple exercises and one more-complex exercise that can be practiced to achieve this goal. Although you might question the ability of one person to sense another person's ki, it is a sixth sense that is developed by successful martial artists. Not only does this ability allow them to sense attacks at an earlier time, but it also provides them with a better-than-average ability to sense danger and possibly avoid it. Some people call it "a greater awareness of one's surroundings."

The first exercise requires only two people: the tori and the uke. The tori assumes an informal sitting position with back straight, eyes closed and hands palm-down on his thighs. The uke sits across from him, also in an informal position. Once the tori is relaxed, he raises his hands to chest height, holding them several inches apart with the palms facing each other and his fingers facing the uke. The uke then slowly passes one of his hands between the hands of the tori. If the tori thinks he senses or "feels" the hand of the uke, he is to slowly bring his hands together, but not touch them. If his hands touch, he must put them palm-down on his thighs and start over again. The tori will initially bring his hands together quite frequently even though the uke has not brought his hand between the hands of the tori. Eventually, with practice, the tori will become more

35

successful at sensing when the hand of the tori is actually passing through his hands. This exercise must be practiced in absolute silence.

The second exercise is very similar to the first, but it requires three to four people. In this exercise, the tori is in a *tachi waza* (standing ready position) with eyes either closed (preferable) or covered. The two to three uke stand around him. Once the tori is in a relaxed state of mind, he should indicate such by nodding his head. Each uke should slowly reach out toward him one at a time in random sequence. If the tori senses or feels movement toward him, he should slowly turn and block in the direction of the sensed reach. Again, this activity must be done very slowly and in absolute silence to be effective.

The third exercise involves executing jujitsu or soft-art techniques on an uke while you, the tori, are blindfolded. Whereas the first two exercises can be done by students at all levels, this exercise should be limited to *sankyu* (three steps below first-degree black belt) and higher-ranking students—ones who have a good working knowledge of the basic kata and waza of their art.

Attacks should be performed slowly and limited to grabs and chokes. Shioku waza techniques should also be executed slowly. This is an excellent exercise to develop an awareness of the other person's ki and how both of your bodies move during an effectively executed shioku waza, as well as where your opponent will end up. The lack of outside distractions helps you develop an excellent awareness of your attacker. Most importantly, it will improve your ability to center your ki. (Centering ki is an absolute necessity in perfecting shioku waza and executing self-defense techniques for maximum effectiveness.) Ideally, this exercise should be done in silence for optimal benefit.

All martial arts are designed for self-improvement. Some martial arts, such as jujitsu, are more effective for street self-defense than others. However, you must be in a state of mushin for any martial art to be effective in a street situation. You must relax to the point where your entire mind can subconsciously deal with the current threat, perceive the immediate environment and assess the danger facing you. If you are in a state of mushin, you can handle a street confrontation successfully, whether it be talking your way out of the situation or, if necessary, physically protecting yourself from injury.

If you are a sensei who wants your students to develop a useful self-defense system, it is essential that you develop their skills in reaching a state of mushin. Students need to develop this skill through continuous practice in a dojo (if one is available). Kata is extremely important and provides a firm foundation for everything else in the martial arts. However, kata is of no value on the street if the student hasn't even been able to mentally condition himself for self-defense in a supervised situation.

Kuzushi

Ki and mushin are two essential elements in developing a strong working knowledge of shioku waza or any martial art. There is a third element which also needs to be understood: kuzushi (balance). It is the essential element that makes it possible for you to use your ki effectively from a state of mushin. If you have centered your ki and are well-balanced during the execution of a technique, this means your kuzushi is good and the maneuver will be successful. If you are off balance, or your thoughts are elsewhere, you will not have kuzushi and thus will be unable to execute a technique to the best of your ability.

Conversely, it is absolutely necessary to destroy the kuzushi of your opponent if you plan to execute techniques properly, whether in kata practice or a street situation. All you need to do to destroy a person's kuzushi is create a distraction. That distraction may be a verbalization such as "Your zipper is down," "Your shoe is untied," "Look out!" or "Who's behind you?" Any simple phrase will do. It can also be a very slight body movement on your part designed to distract him, such as moving one or two of your fingers. A light tap on the ear or nose can also serve as a distraction. Lastly, the distraction may be an attack to a nerve center using thumb or finger pressure.

Such distractions will work only momentarily (with the exception of a nerve attack, in which the pain can be maintained by continuing pressure on the nerve center), so it is essential that you execute a defensive technique immediately following the distraction. These distractions will upset his kuzushi for 0.3 to 0.7 seconds—the time it takes for the brain to register the distraction and his body to react to it. Even a light strike to his solar plexus will work.

You can also destroy your opponent's kuzushi in two more serious manners, both of which are very difficult to recover from quickly. First, you can hit or kick your opponent in a sensitive area or nerve center with a great deal of force. A strong hit or kick may sufficiently debilitate an attacker, not only destroying his kuzushi but making it impossible for him to continue his assault, thus making it unnecessary for you to do anything further.

The second method of destroying an attacker's kuzushi is by using his ki against him. In this manner, you "help" the attacker by continuing his body movement in the direction that he initiated. The use of pressure on nerve-center points can also assist you in this method. Assuming your ki is centered, you could then redirect his ki in a circular motion, thus bringing your opponent down with a throw or by placing him in a hold.

For example, if your assailant strikes at you with a right fist, you can move your body to your right as you deflect his hit to your left with your right forearm, allowing his momentum to continue. Your right middle finger then presses or strikes a nerve in the left side of his neck (from his perspective). At the same time, your left hand grabs his right forearm. Continue the pressure on the nerve in his neck as you pull his right arm and continue to pivot out of the way to his left, thus executing a circular throw and bringing him down to the ground. In essence, you have helped the attacker go where he wants to go by getting out of his way while you redirect and guide his ki.

Conclusions

What makes it possible for you to have control over your attacker? It's your ability to control the ki and kuzushi of both you and your attacker. Executing techniques from a state of mushin also develops this skill.

How can you effectively protect yourself and yet not find it necessary to destroy your assailant in the process? As a skilled practitioner, you have a wide variety of techniques to use in any given situation, thus providing the advantage of unpredictability. Because all of these techniques have been used on you during training, you also have a very good understanding of how they will affect an attacker in terms of pain, control and injury potential, as well as where your opponent will end up when the technique is completed. Part of the jujitsu philosophy is to do only what is necessary to remove oneself from danger. Lastly, you develop a sixth sense that helps you form a greater awareness of your immediate environment and current situation.

Using all of these factors makes it possible for you to act responsibly in terms of protecting yourself. Excessive force becomes unnecessary because you know what the techniques can do. Hopefully, you will automatically choose an appropriate response to a given attack. That's a tall order, but it's part of the responsibility of being a skilled jujitsu practitioner.

What advantage do you as a jujitsu practitioner possess that may be neglected or not stressed in other martial arts? As one top jujitsu *yudansha*

Pain vs. Injury

Pain is a non-specific term for a signal transmitted via the central nervous system from the point of contact to the cortex of your brain which indicates an unpleasant sensation caused by injury to (or a functional disorder in) a particular part of the body. It is your body's initial reaction to unpleasant nerve stimuli. It takes your nervous system approximately 0.3 to 0.7 seconds to react with a reflex action via nerves and to notify your brain that there is pain somewhere. Within the context of this book, pain is caused by cellular injury (and/or damage) or by pressure on nerves, pressure points and nerve centers.

For self-defense purposes, you can execute techniques against an assailant for the purpose of creating pain. You can use pain to secure a release from a hold, for purposes of intimidation, to prevent further attack by an assailant, or to secure compliance and cooperation. If necessary, pain can be used to inflict short- or long-term injury to an assailant if it is a life-or-death situation. If used irresponsibly, pain can also be used to generate techniques which may maim or kill an assailant by either sharp blows to sensitive parts of the body or by causing an assailant to go into shock (which can be fatal in and of itself) as a result of the sustained injuries.

There are also different intensity levels of pain that can be used, depending on your goal. However, the amount of pain you create must be serious enough to, at the very least, cause the assailant to suffer enough discomfort to release a hold or cease his attack. The application of techniques that cause pain can also be intense enough to cause minor to major injury to the assailant, depending on the severity of the attack and the situation in which you find yourself.

Pain compliance is a concept that is different from the simple concept of creating pain to end an attack. The purpose of pain compliance is to establish control over an attacker with minimal or no injury taking place by applying pressure to nerve centers to short-circuit the nervous system. It aims to use pain to secure cooperation via nerve/pressure points or joint locking/hyperextension before any injury actually takes place. As a result, pain-compliance techniques are very suitable to martial artists and law-enforcement personnel who wish to use the least amount of force necessary to protect themselves and control assailants.

If you can accept the concept of pain compliance as a viable tool within your martial arts training, then you can also accept the concept that pain has no value if it has no goal or purpose except to inflict suffering or physical damage. The ability to control the amount of pain delivered to your assailant without injuring him will give you a tremendous advantage on the street.

Pain and the Martial Arts

Each martial art and ryu has particular characteristics, strengths and weaknesses. It would be impossible to delineate these characteristics for every art and ryu; the comparison chart would be endless since different ryu crop up every day, especially in the United States. However, for the sake of providing a background, it is possible to list the major attributes of the three *do* (way[s]) that make up most ryu of jujitsu. It is historically established that jujitsu is the parent art of judo, aikido and some karate ryu. Each of these do have their own distinct attributes, which gives jujitsu its major strength and advantage: flexibility.

Judo (ju = gentle, do = way) is composed of throws and sweeps which cause an assailant to impact upon the ground. Throws can cause fractures, sprains and concussions. The pins, chokes, and hold-downs used in judo for the purpose of immobilization can cause fractures, sprains and dislocations—as well as loss of consciousness—when used on an untrained attacker.

Karate (a.k.a. karatedo; *kara* = empty, *te* = hand, *do* = way) is composed mainly of a series of strikes, hits and kicks. These actions can cause body-to-body impact injuries such as fractures, concussions, serious contusions and internal damage.

Techniques that involve locking and hyperextending joints, as well as the use of the attacker's momentum (ki), comprise the basis for most aikido (*ai* = mind, ki = spirit, do = way) techniques. The use of aikido techniques for self-defense can cause joint injuries, including fractures, dislocations and severe joint-tissue damage. These are in addition to injuries sustained by an attacker when he hits the ground. Some aikido ryu are very "soft," which is to say they will even bring the attacker down to the ground with care whenever possible. Aikido techniques may also make use of nerves and pressure points (a.k.a. controlled pain) for the purpose of pain compliance. Aikido could be considered one of the "softest" martial arts because of its maximized use of the attacker's ki and circular movements to keep him off balance.

All three of these do are integrated in jujitsu. This gives you the advantage of being unpredictable when defending yourself. It also makes jujitsu well-suited to the use of pain-compliance techniques that utilize atemi waza for the purpose of executing shioku waza.

If you are in a sound and well-structured instructional program, you will learn about pain compliance relatively early in your white-belt (beginner) training. You will also begin to learn about human anatomy and kinesthetics (body movement). Lastly, but most important, you will be introduced to a very strong philosophy of non-violence. This philosophy includes the acceptance of some basic guidelines:

- A physical conflict should be avoided whenever possible, as such a conflict means that all human reason has failed. It is degrading to be involved in a physical confrontation, regardless of the outcome.

- A competent jujitsu practitioner has a responsibility to his attacker if a physical conflict should occur: He is to respond to an attack without using excessive force or employing his technical skills beyond what is necessary.

Pain-compliance techniques allow you to use pain rather than injury to secure cooperation and end an attack. This does not mean that injuring an attacker can always be avoided; however, it does give you a more flexible advantage in defending yourself. Because you are acting responsibly to the best of your ability, there is no conflict with the philosophy of non-violence. In fact, the philosophy of non-violence is actually enhanced because the intent is to control the attacker without injuring him.

Jujitsu training gives you the ability to use a variety of techniques designed to establish control via less-than-equal force. It is therefore less likely that you will have to deal with the issue of excessive force should any legal questions arise. Pain-compliance techniques allow for good control of an attacker because once a hold is set, resistance from the attacker will provoke a response of additional pressure on his nerves or joints—and thus more pain.

In addition, if you use a leverage hold, you won't have to apply additional force against the attacker. The level of pain is controlled by the person maintaining the hold, as he is aware of the pain level at hand by the attacker's reaction to his shioku waza. The attacker may quickly learn that increased resistance to such a hold will result in increased pain, thus realizing it may be to his advantage to cease resistance and become cooperative and submissive to his intended victim.

All shioku waza can cause serious injury, but they usually allow for a great deal of joint manipulation and varying levels of pain before serious injury occurs. Within the same framework, hits to joints can be used as distractions to cause an assailant to lose his balance and drop to the ground in a controlled manner. Many pain-compliance techniques are relatively easy to teach and extremely effective. As a result, they are ideal for law-enforcement personnel to use because they reduce the level of force required to subdue a suspect.

Conclusions

Pain-compliance techniques are an effective way to control an assailant without excessive force. They allow you to vary the level of pain as necessary to secure the cooperation of the assailant without the need to inflict injury. As a result, only minimal force is usually required to secure and maintain control over an attacker.

The martial art of jujitsu is uniquely suited to the use of pain-compliance techniques because properly trained practitioners develop an understanding of the human anatomy, nerves and body movement. As jujitsu is a parent art (containing the knowledge of judo, karatedo and aikido), learning techniques that integrate the movements of the three do makes you better able to execute the effective atemi waza and shioku waza that are essential to control an attacker. Also, because pain-compliance techniques reduce the level of violence, they are more philosophically, morally and legally acceptable in general.

CHAPTER 4

OW!
RELIEVING THE ANGST
OF PRESSURE-POINT
TRAINING

T he assailant swings at you. You move out of the way, deflect his fist to your right and move behind him. Suddenly, your left middle finger presses down on the supraclavicular or auricular nerve at the base of his neck and he's down. The stunning pain is sudden and swift, but momentary. The assailant may not really be hurt, although he may be disoriented. There are no marks on his body from your touch and you haven't even used "equal" force to protect yourself.

What happened? Was it a secret technique taught only to masters at some ancient Asian temple? Did you have a stun gun hidden in your hand? Did you strike him with a *shuto* (edge of the hand)? No, none of these! The attacker's neck and shoulder area cried out, "I'm easily available and there are lots of pressure points you can use—just pick one and press!"

The use of pressure points (a.k.a. impact points, attack points, vital points, acupressure points or chi meridian points) and balance points in the martial arts is a very sensitive issue (no pun intended). Some arts and ryu restrict instruction of this subject to upper belts, sometimes starting with instruction only after the student has reached the rank of yudansha. Pressure points may be considered secret techniques to be taught only at the higher black belt levels or from an older sensei to his hopeful successors. Other arts and ryu provide instruction in this area concurrent with the student's growth and proficiency, sometimes even starting at the white belt (beginner level). So much for secret techniques.

In budoshin jujitsu, you should start learning pressure points and balance points from the outset of your training. The original 43 basic pressure points can be found in *Jujitsu: Basic Techniques of the Gentle Art* (Kirby, 1983). How long will it take students to learn the 43 points? By the time they're sankyu, the students will know most of them by osmosis—much like all the other kata and waza they've learned. They will have been exposed to pressure points and practiced using them so many times that their presence and technical applicability become almost second nature. By the time a student reaches *shodan* (first-degree black belt), he will probably have a working knowledge of most of the 100 basic points on the human body (actually 182 points if you include both sides of the head, body and extremities). Many of these points can be cross-referenced to acupressure (chi meridian) points, trigger points (Western massage) and particular nerves or nerve centers.

Effective application of pressure-point techniques can give you absolute control over an attacker through pain rather than injury, although injury can easily occur. This is why pressure-point training must be done with caution and consideration for your workout partner.

There is a certain amount of angst among students when pressure points are practiced in the dojo. Much of this anxiety is caused by the anticipation and fear of pain. Shioku waza does tend to be a bit nerve-wracking (another pun not intended) because students practice on each other. However, it need not be an overly painful or debilitating experience. It can be carried out in relative safety, yielding positive results for sensei and student alike. To reduce angst and facilitate a positive learning experience, there are 10 guidelines that should be followed to maximize effective learning of the use of pressure and balance points:

1. Practicing Pressure Points

You cannot practice pressure-point techniques repeatedly, regardless of how gentle you are. A single technique can usually be practiced only one to three times before your partner becomes intolerant of the discomfort and resistant to any shioku waza, which will only cause him greater discomfort. This will occur even if you apply light pressure to a given point. In addition, your partner will not want to have any other pressure-point techniques practiced on him after reaching his tolerance threshold. Therefore, pain, regardless of how slight, may be intolerable. If you are working out continuously with pressure points, you will have to find another partner after 1 or 2 minutes. That's why it's better to intersperse pressure-point techniques with other types of practice, limiting a class to only two to three pressure-point maneuvers per 1- to 2-hour workout period.

2. Be Considerate to Your Partner in Practice

When working out with your partner, it is very important to be considerate. You should apply only the minimal amount of pressure necessary to secure his cooperation. Keep in mind that your partner will be practicing on you, too, so you can experience what the pressure point feels like. It is also courteous to massage around the area of the pressure point (away from the heart) after you have applied pressure. If you used a nerve in your partner's neck, massage downward (away from the head). Not only does this help relax the surrounding muscles and relieve soreness, but it also helps restore your partner's ki. Remember the standard rule in jujitsu: You have a responsibility to take care of your partner and protect him from injury.

3. Human Physiology

To use pressure points effectively, you must have a basic understanding of human physiology. We're all basically built the same, feel the same kind of stimuli, and innately react the same way out of instinct: Get away from pain. Figuratively speaking, you have to be able to see through your partner's *gi* (uniform) or other clothing. You should be able to put a hand on your opponent's body and find the nearest pressure point relatively quickly without looking or grabbing around for the right spot. You won't have that luxury on the street. In some cases, you may have to go through two to three layers of heavy clothing. The advantage of wearing a judo gi is that it requires the student to apply pressure through moderately thick clothing. Furthermore, the gi or other clothing forces the student to visualize the human body (and where its pressure points are) through clothing rather than letting him look at bare body parts to find the correct spot.

4. Develop Technique Sensitivity

By working with a partner, you will develop a sensitivity to techniques involving various pressure points. Such role-trading will help you develop the ability to sense what pain you are inflicting upon your opponent by how your own body moves and reacts to stimuli. You will soon develop the ability to vary the amount of pressure you apply to a pressure point, depending on the situation and your needs. In essence, you will develop the ability to determine how much pain the opponent will receive, how he will react and what the consequences will be. Pain compliance is an important skill in effective self-defense that can and must be fine-tuned for maximum effectiveness on the street.

5. Ki and Kuzushi

It is extremely important to recognize that your ki and kuzushi must be as relaxed and balanced as possible for pressure and balance points to be used to their maximum potential. This is very critical when you are using direct or manipulative pressure rather than an impact strike. With an impact strike, your goal is to create an immediate but momentary stun or pain reaction. Although proper and accurate targeting is required for this, you will not be maintaining contact with the attacker. With direct or manipulative pressure, the goal is control through the use of pain. You must be balanced and relaxed so that you can sense your assailant's movements and reactions to your pressure. Then you must compensate for them so as to maintain pressure on the pressure point you are using.

In the case of balance points, maintaining your balance allows you to control your attacker's balance as you guide him in the direction you wish. Keeping yourself as relaxed as possible also makes it possible for

Because it is painful, there is a lot of angst attached to pressure-point training. Learning what pain can do is an arduous process. Students are hesitant to practice pressure-point techniques because of the real and imagined pain involved in the process of perfecting their usage. However, by following the 10 guidelines presented here, the students' angst can be minimized. In so doing, learning can become a positive experience for tori and uke alike.

The use of pressure points through direct or manipulative pressure will provide you with an alternative for defending yourself. It gives you another choice, another option and another direction. Within the spirit of budo, you do have a responsibility to your attacker. Through the skillful use of pressure points, you can effectively and efficiently defend yourself within the guidelines of the budo discipline.

CHAPTER 5

CHANGE: FOUNDATIONS, TRADITIONS AND PEDESTALS

T he only thing permanent is *change*. Change is inevitable. Change is for the good. If you can't change, then history will leave you in its tracks.

You need a good *foundation* to do anything. A sound building requires a solid foundation. A good foundation is the cornerstone of all knowledge.

Tradition! This is the way previous generations have lived—as should you. Tradition is security. Tradition is safe. The traditional way is the right and only way.

Which idea is right? Is there really a conflict between tradition and change? In this conflict, do we create false pedestals upon which we place objects to be revered? Or is change inevitable and tradition simply part of the process? Utilizing the knowledge you gain from this book may raise these and other questions.

Foundations

In order to grow in any martial art, you must start with a firm foundation—a base upon which everything else is built. This requires a commitment on your part. While it may take a certain amount of time and searching to find the right combination, you must make a commitment to yourself at some point to learn a particular art or ryu and work under a particular sensei. There is nothing wrong with exploring different martial arts, ryu and sensei to find out which one is best suited to your needs. This exploration may result in some moving around, the amount of which usually depends on whether or not you understand your capabilities and know what you want.

You should also realize that you must have a willingness to give up part of your life to learn something that will change it forever if you take the task seriously. Therefore, part of your ultimate commitment must be to trust that your sensei will act in your best interest within the foundations and traditions of his particular martial art. Knowing these things can expedite your search. Once you seriously get into one martial art, you may find that your goals have changed and a particular ryu or sensei can no longer help you reach them. However, if you constantly change arts, ryu and sensei, you will learn nothing of substance.

Also keep in mind that changes in your goals usually come about as a result of the philosophical direction in which your art takes you. My initial goal in studying jujitsu was to learn a form of relaxation and have a distraction while I was studying for my master's degree at California State University, Los Angeles. Ironically, my goal did not involve becoming a sensei, nor did it include making jujitsu such a large part of my life. That just happened as the process evolved, situations changed and opportunities opened up for me.

You must think of the commitment you make to a particular art, ryu or sensei in terms of years (or as long as it takes to develop a solid foundation in that particular art). I usually tell my serious students that they shouldn't study another martial art or ryu until they achieve brown belt (about 2 years from the start of training) or black belt (about 3 to 7 years from the start of training). Why? Because it will take them that long to develop a secure foundation in jujitsu. The 2- to 7-year time period will give students the opportunity to not only learn the basics of the art, but also start to learn the art itself by going through the five-step learning process: patience, repetition, understanding, experimentation and evaluation.[3]

1. Exploration: Once you have gone through this five-step process, two things will occur. First, once the foundation is established, you can really start to grow and advance in your chosen art. You may then experiment with various techniques, striving to improve or modify them to work more efficiently both independently and in different combinations. After Sensei Seki promoted me to shodan, he said, "Now you are ready to learn." At that time, I don't think I fully understood the implications of what he said. Thirty years later, he is still right; I am still learning the art.

I have found that most of my students start going through this process once they reach the second or first *kyu* (level below black belt). By this time, you will have learned many of the 30 to 50 basic techniques in jujitsu. The process then becomes extremely intense as they progress through the early yudansha grades of shodan and *nidan* (second-degree black belt). Students eventually devise valid variations of techniques I teach them. This happens in any martial art; it is part of the learning process.

In studying and evaluating what you are doing, you may actually be validating what you have already learned. You may also be sowing some roots of change; in fact, you may believe such change will end up challenging tradition. Whether or not you intentionally choose to do so, your knowledge and the processes you are going through will serve as the tools for change over a number of years or even generations. This is when a martial art becomes your life and you eventually become a "master" of its practice by developing a thorough understanding of its many nuances.

---

3. George Kirby, *Jujitsu: Intermediate Techniques of the Gentle Art*, (Burbank: Ohara Publications, Inc., 1985), 28-29.

2. Expansion: The second outcome of a firm foundation is that you can start to learn a second martial art (if you choose to do so) without being confronted by insurmountable technique conflicts. Once you have a firm foundation in one art, learning a second art may be like learning a new and different skill and going through the five-step learning process again. However, regardless of your conscious wishes, this time you will find yourself applying the knowledge of the first martial art you learned to the second one.

Knowledge is cumulative and change is unavoidable! You will inevitably blend components of the two arts into something that works best for you. You are building upon a firm foundation at this point; and what you are building may be a strong structure for supporting additional growth and change. You may end up creating a hybrid art that is viable not only for you but for the general population. If you have developed a firm foundation in your parent martial art (in which you hopefully advance into the black belt grades), you may add elements of other arts to your repertoire and integrate them into your original art, thus modifying or changing your parent ryu.

At this point, you will be confronted with the issue that faces all of us in the martial arts: *If I modify or change a technique, what will my sensei think of me? If I make changes in the ryu that I have been taught, am I making a break with tradition?*

Tradition

Tradition is the word with which every student in every martial art is eventually confronted:

"These are the traditions of our ryu."

"This is the traditional way the kata (or waza) is performed."

"Your sensei is preserving the traditions and expects you to follow in his footsteps."

In many dojo, students learn about traditions regarding courtesy and respect in their very first class. Tradition has earned a bad rap in martial arts because we, as martial artists, have given tradition a specific and very limiting definition. It has come to indicate that things should be done today as they were in the past, meaning if an *ippon seoi nage* (one-arm hip throw) was done one way by a sensei several generations ago, that is the correct and only way to execute it. That's how the technique will be taught in the dojo and that's how you will be expected to learn and perfect it so you can teach it to your students someday. It's a lock-step process.

Pedestals

Pedestals are terrific places to display art objects. When you put an *objet d'art* (art object) on a pedestal, it means you are giving it a place of prominence. It becomes something to be admired, revered and reflected upon. It is also static. It neither moves nor evolves; therefore, it does not change. While a piece of art may look fine on a pedestal, to place a martial art, sensei or—worst of all—yourself on such a pedestal is to court disaster.

When something is placed on a pedestal, it is placed there because it is something that is unobtainable or nearly so. Martial arts evolve. Sensei change. Students come and go. It seems somewhat contradictory that any one of these should be placed upon a pedestal. There is nothing wrong with respecting yourself, your sensei or your art and honoring its traditions. However, if you place any one of these on a pedestal, you are inferring that they don't move, don't evolve or don't change.

Placing an art, sensei or oneself on a pedestal also creates the illusion of superiority. This can result in an arrogant attitude that directly violates the martial arts' concepts of respect, integrity and humility. Rather than respect, an attitude of arrogance spawns resentment by others. Rather than integrity, an attitude of arrogance creates a feeling of hostility among others. Instead of humility, an attitude of arrogance results in disrespect from others. Those around you can and will sense your lack of respect and your air of arrogance, regardless of how you try to conceal or deny it.

The basic problem with placing things on pedestals is they can be knocked over quite easily. If you place your art, sensei or yourself on a pedestal, you are setting yourself up for a fall. Remember that art objects break when they fall off pedestals—and they can't be glued back together. Arrogance is like a double-edged sword; it cuts both ways. This is the really sad part of the whole process.

A problem with placing things, ideas and people—especially yourself—on pedestals is that doing so will usually cause you to lose sight of your foundation because you can't see your base. You may also lose sight of the traditions that support the foundation upon which the pedestal stands. As you assume an attitude of arrogance, you may also lose contact with—and the respect of—those who helped you along your path of learning. The ultimate loss may be sight of the path to a better understanding of your art, its foundation and its traditions, as well as a true appreciation of your sensei.

If you display arrogance and disregard the foundation and traditions of your parent art and sensei, the final loss can be traumatic. You may end up isolating yourself from the mainstream. Your new circle of associates may ultimately lose respect for you and dwindle in number as they realize you have placed yourself on a pedestal. You place yourself, your art or your sensei on a pedestal only if you seek to establish a false sense of security (and possibly, in the case of a sensei, blind obedience). When the bubble bursts, respect and integrity are lost.

Conclusions

Wow! There really are some conflicts here. Foundations provide integrity. Traditions enhance foundations. The concept of change challenges both. Who is right? Is there really a conflict between tradition and change? In the process of this conflict, do we create false pedestals upon which to place objects for reverence? Or is change inevitable and tradition simply part of the process?

Throughout history, numerous philosophers have dealt with the inevitability of change. Many suggest that in order to survive the inevitability of change, you must have a basic core of values that will allow you to function in an ever-changing environment. This concept can be applied to the martial arts. The basic core of values comes from the foundation of your art and the traditions it encompasses. If you have a sound foundation and sense of tradition, the art will survive and you will thrive as a martial artist. If the system you studied is viable, it will survive because you, as a sensei, will be able to give that foundation to your students. They, in turn, will see the wisdom of the traditions that you honor and practice.

Keep in mind that changes you make in your techniques, etc., will inevitably affect the traditions that surround it. It's what changes you make—and how you implement them—that determine what traditions are kept, altered or ultimately eliminated. Traditions, in order to be valid from the outset, must have some purpose beyond mere surface protocol. Ideally, their purpose should be philosophical or altruistic rather than physical or material.

Is there a single right answer to all of this debate? Probably not. It is possible to say that a sound foundation and viable traditions are essential if you wish to implement change that will survive. It is also essential to understand that any changes which disregard a sound foundation and tradition will not survive once their progenitor ceases to be their active proponent (whether through conceptual abandonment or physical death).

In studying any martial art, it is important you realize that it will take perhaps 10 to 20 years (or longer) to establish a firm foundation and understanding of your chosen martial art's traditions. For many serious martial artists, learning a single art can be a lifelong journey. With such a strong foundation and acceptance of the traditions of your art, you will inevitably make changes to it. Simply by walking the path, you will change it. The changes you make will usually be small, but they can clear the path for those who follow in your footsteps.

For example, if you were doing research and made a discovery or changed a process for the better, you have modified the "footing on the path." The next time around, either you or a colleague will have an easier time proceeding forward. Likewise, when you change how a technique is taught, you may simplify it for your students. When doing either, you are changing the mechanics of the move or task being performed. You may be changing the structure, but the foundation and traditions remain—for that *is* the art.

CHAPTER 6

BRINGING IT ALL TOGETHER

Shioku waza is an important skill in jujitsu and any martial art. To be proficient in the use of shioku waza, you must be skilled in atemi waza. You must be able to locate and use vital points on the human body to disorient an attacker and secure control so that you can execute shioku waza. As previously discussed, this requires a sound knowledge of human physiology and kinesthetics plus long-term practice. The goal is to develop a sensitivity toward the techniques you use and an understanding of how they're affecting the attacker.

To effectively protect yourself from street attacks by using shioku waza, you must be able to redirect your attacker's ki while maintaining your own. You must preserve your kuzushi to execute techniques satisfactorily and maintain control over your attacker. You must also be able to operate from a state of mushin, in which no conscious effort is going into your defensive moves. It's a matter of automatic reactions while maintaining good judgment in executing techniques. Shioku waza will work only if these conditions prevail.

To properly implement shioku waza, you must also have an understanding of how pain can be used to control an attacker, that pain and injury are two different things, and that your goal should be to avoid injuring an attacker if possible. By practicing shioku waza (as both a tori and an uke), you will develop a sensitivity to how shioku waza can affect the human body. However, training in its use can be very painful unless you follow certain guidelines in practice. Following the guidelines presented in this book will help you learn shioku waza effectively without causing undue pain or discomfort to your uke in practice.

Lastly, regardless of your martial art, you may find that you change the way you execute techniques once you start using shioku waza. How you deal with the consequences of the changes it makes in your art depends on you, your belief in what you have previously learned, and whether or not you're capable of handling the changes shioku waza may make in your self-defense system. In some cases, using shioku waza will enhance your ryu. In other cases, it may raise major questions about the traditional way of doing things—and there may be conflicts that arise out of your new knowledge. Hopefully, this book has provided some tools to help you deal with the issues of tradition and change.

Most importantly, however, shioku waza will hopefully allow you to defend yourself more effectively while using a lower level of force. Establishing control over an assailant is the most important goal of shioku waza. By establishing control over an attacker, the need to injure him is reduced. As a result, you will be a more effective and philosophically grounded martial artist.

Shioku waza will allow you to be more at peace with yourself and minimize the scope of a physical altercation should you have to defend yourself. A physical confrontation occurs due to the failure of all rational means of intellectual negotiation and is the most degrading event in which a martial artist can become involved. It means you must resort to physical rather than mental skills to protect yourself, which can be construed as a failure from the philosophical standpoint. While being recognized as ultimately necessary, using a martial art to defend yourself still demeans it. After all, the purpose of learning a martial art is to avoid physical conflict because it is unnecessary if rational minds prevail. During such an encounter, the issue is no longer whether you merely defend yourself, but how you control your attacker. It becomes a matter of using your ki, mushin and kuzushi to protect yourself and your attacker from unnecessary injury, thus maintaining the tenets of the original philosophy even while in the throes of physical conflict.

As you work through the techniques presented in this book, keep those concepts in mind. Try to learn the techniques as an art, which is the way they should ideally work. Also, practice them in realistic self-defense situations. Practicing techniques from any martial art in this two-pronged approach will not only make you a better student, but ultimately a better sensei.

Safety Guidelines

- Always practice in a safe, quiet environment. Noise and other distractions can be your greatest safety hazard.

- Use high-quality mats. At minimum, your practice area should be 8 feet by 8 feet. Wear loose clothing. A judo gi is preferred (because it will withstand abuse), but it is not required.

- Practice techniques smoothly and slowly, even as you become more proficient. If you execute techniques smoothly, speed will come naturally. Executing them quickly can result in serious, permanent injury to your workout partner. Remember that you should be learning to control your assailant via the minimum amount of pain necessary to attain compliance.

- Become sensitive to your partner's reactions and body movements as you apply pressure to nerves or pressure points. Learn to use the minimum amount of pressure necessary to secure cooperation so you can do what you want to do. (This is part of the "minimal use of force" concept.)

- Immediately cease any hold, technique, nerve or pressure-point use, submission or lock if your partner indicates submission. (Such an indication might come in the form of him saying, *"Maitta,"* which means "to give up.")

- Practice a specific nerve- or pressure-point attack no more than two to three times maximum per session because the body is very sensitive to these. Also, as a matter of courtesy, once you have executed a nerve or pressure-point technique, massage the area away from the heart to reduce sensitivity or discomfort. If you used a nerve in the neck or shoulder, massage away from the head.

- While the jujitsu techniques shown in this book use particular nerves, pressure points and balance points, please be aware that they can also be used with techniques not shown in this book. They may also work well independently without supplemental techniques. If you choose to practice these techniques with different attacks, do so carefully as proficiency is gradually achieved.

- Use good judgment when defending yourself on the street. In a street situation, you are usually allowed to use only the amount of force necessary to remove yourself from the situation and protect yourself from injury. These are vague terms which may be interpreted in the courtroom. Be as conservative as possible when using your martial arts training in real-life situations so as to protect yourself from legal ramifications.

- Review the other safety factors and elements of consideration in Chapter 4.

CHAPTER 7

PRESSURE-POINT TECHNIQUES

Technique 1:
Winding Strike Attack
(Makikomi Shioku Waza)

Submission:	None
Attack:	Lapel Grab
Pressure Points:	36, 50

Ready position.

Attacker grabs your lapel with right hand.

Your left hand comes up (palm up) under his right elbow...

...raising it up as you step under his arm...

...and stay next to his right side as you step, keeping hip to hip.

Strike his right kidney at point 50 (thoracic nerve) with your right elbow.

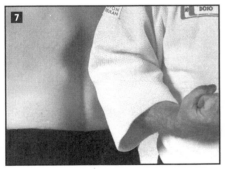

Close-up of kidney strike.

Turn to your left on the balls of your feet.

Strike attacker's side at the base of his ribs (floating ribs) at point 36 (intercostal nerve) with left elbow.

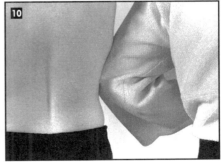

Close-up of rib strike.

Front view of rib strike.

Step back into ready position behind the attacker.

Technique 2:
Elbow-Roll Takedown
(Heiji No Maki)

Submission:	Wrist-Press Arm-Pin (Tekubi Shimi Waza)
Attack:	Rear Waist Grab
Pressure Points:	58, 75

Attacker sets rear waist grab.

Your right hand comes up and presses point 58 (radial nerve) between the thumb and index finger of his right hand.

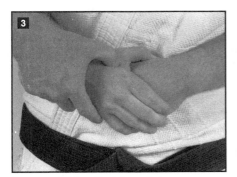

Proper point for attack to radial nerve.

Slide his right hand down to your right side (without pulling it away from you) as you start to turn to your right.

Maintain pressure on point 58 as you raise his arm up, bending the wrist so the palm is facing up.

Continue to step around to your right side so you're facing the same direction (as in next photo).

Come up under the backside of his arm (just above his elbow) to bend it so the elbow is facing upward.

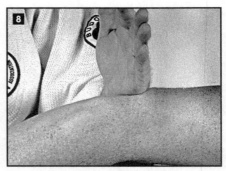

Keeping his arm slightly bent (makes the elbow roll easier and more effective), place your left forearm (near your wrist) on the inner backside of his upper arm, just above the elbow.

Roll your arm forward to roll his arm and bring him face-down.

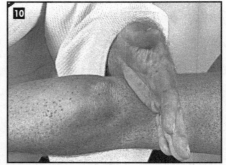

If you let your hand relax downward, the technique works better because your ki is more effectively directed.

If the attacker rolls forward so he ends face-up...

...move in to set a wrist-press and...

...drop your left knee down on his upper arm at point 75 (ulnar nerve, about one-third of the way up from his elbow) to complete the submission.

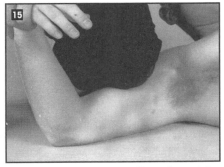

Wrist-press and proper position of your left knee.

Technique 3:
Nerve Attack Rear Throw
(Shioku Ashi Nage Ushiro)

Submission: None
Attack: Head Lock
Pressure Points: 19, 95

Attacker places you in a head lock.

Bring your right hand up; your right middle finger presses point 19 (supraclavicular nerve) near the base of the right side of his neck.

Proper placement of right middle finger at point 19.

Immediately after pressing point 19, tuck your chin in toward your chest and press point 95 (tibial nerve) at the back of his left knee, lifting the leg.

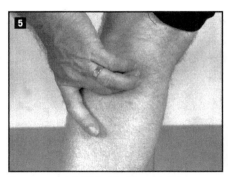

Pressure point 95 behind knee joint.

Pivot your right leg back and go down on your right knee as you bring him down, keeping your head against his chest.

Technique 4:
Throat Attack Takedown
(Nozo Shioku Waza)

Submission: (Included as part of takedown.)
Attack: Lapel Grab
Pressure Points: 21

Ready position.

Attacker grabs you...

...and pulls you to him.

Grab high on both of his lapels and...

Technique 6:
Submission for Striking
Attack with Ear-Press

Submission: Ear-Press Submission (Mimi Shioku Waza)
Attack: Knife Thrust
Pressure Points: 7, 21

*Note: The following sequence is part of the "complete formal kata" for the previous striking attack, but the knife slice is **NOT** appropriate for street use.*

After securing the knife from your attacker, drop down and rest your left kneecap on point 7 (right ear). Shift your body weight to your left kneecap for pain compliance. *(**Option:** Place knife against the right side of attacker's neck.)*

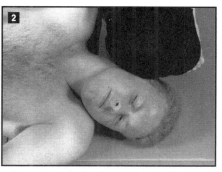

Left knee on attacker's ear at point 7.

Pull knife across neck and cut. *(**Note:** This is for demonstrating a complete kata. Cutting a person's neck in a street situation will probably be considered excessive force and put YOU in jail!)*

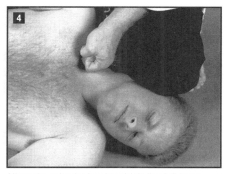

Alternate submission in which the left knee presses down on point 7 (right ear) for *mimi shioku waza* while the left fist is clenched into a gingitzu, pressing down on point 21 (phrenic nerve, located at the base of neck near artery toward front).

83

Technique 7:
Neck Nerve Attack Rear Takedown
(Kubi Shioku Ushiru Waza)

Submission: Wrist-Lock Press (Tekubi Shimi Waza)
Attack: Knife Thrust/Swipe
Pressure Points: 26

Ready position.

Attacker lunges at you with knife in right hand. You aggressively block his forearm with a *juji* (cross-block), simultaneously stepping in as close to him as possible.

Your left forearm continues to block his right arm as you pivot your right foot back clockwise.

Continue blocking with your left arm as your right hand grabs the top of his right wrist (with your right thumb next to his right thumb and the rest of your hand on his hand). Continue to push his hand to his body to get resistance.

Your left hand lets go of block and comes up behind him to press the auricular (or other) nerve at the base of his neck at point 26 (near left shoulder) for distraction.

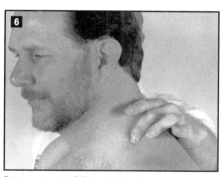

Press at point 26 for distraction.

As attacker reacts to point-26 nerve press, bring knife across his body and up to the left side of his neck as you step in front of him with your right foot.

Shown from rear angle: Continue applying pressure at point 26 as you pivot your left foot back...

...to bring the attacker down.

To complete the formal kata, pull the knife across the neck, cutting it. (***Note:*** *This is for demonstrating a complete kata. Cutting a person's neck in a street situation will probably be considered excessive force and put YOU in jail!*)

85

An alternate submission is to bring the knife hand away from his neck, set a wrist-lock submission...

...and remove the knife from his hand. Snapping the wrist with a wrist-press is an additional submission option.

Technique 8:
Nerve Attack Takedown
(Kubi No Shioku Waza)

Submission: (Included as part of takedown.)
Attack: Waist Grab and Lift
Pressure Points: 25

Ready position.

Attacker moves in, grabbing you around the waist and lifting you off the ground.

As he lifts you, reach behind his head with both hands and press down with your middle fingers at point 25 (occipital nerves) on both sides of his neck.

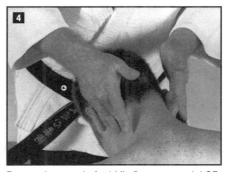

Proper placement of middle fingers on point 25.

87

The pressure application will cause the attacker to release his hold. As you return to the ground, maintain pressure on point 25…

…and bring **him** to the ground.

Make sure he goes **completely** to the ground. Maintain pressure on point 25 for submission.

Technique 9:
Throat Attack Side Throw
(Noso No Shioku Makikomi)

Submission:	Neck Nerve Attack and Strangle (Kubi Shimi Waza)
Attack:	Shirt Grab
Pressure Points:	19

Ready position.

Attacker grabs your right lapel.

Your left hand grabs his right lapel at mid-chest level.

Grab high on his left lapel with your right hand shaped in a gingitzu fist.

Pull his lapel with your left hand, thus causing gingitzu fist to press upon point 19 (at the side of his neck). Steer the attacker to your left as you step in with your right foot.

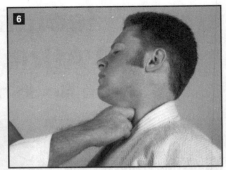

Close-up of gingitzu fist: Clench your fist with your thumb over your index finger and the second knuckle of your middle finger extended.

Continue steering him to your left as you pivot your left foot back counterclockwise, thus throwing him and...

...bringing him to the ground for Neck Nerve Attack and Strangle submission.
(**Note:** *Execute submission* ***carefully***.)

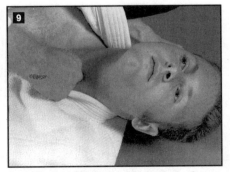

Gingitzu fist is placed against attacker's throat for submission.

Technique 10:
Nerve Attack Hand Throw
(Te No Shioku Nage)

Submission:	Upper Arm Nerve Attack (Ude Tatake)
Attack:	Grab to Opposite Wrist
Pressure Points:	78, 79

Ready position.

Attacker grabs your right wrist.

Your right hand turns clockwise until the back of his hand is facing you and your fingers are pointed to your left. (To make this work, be sure to keep your hand open and relaxed.)

Your left hand comes up and grabs his left wrist. Your left thumb should be pointing toward your right hand, with your left palm facing away from you. Remove your right hand from the attacker's grip.

Step to his left side with your right foot. Turn to face in the same direction as the attacker as...

...your right hand comes up under his upper arm at point 79 with a knife-edge right hand and rolls it, bending his elbow.

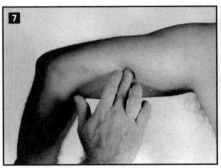

Knife-edge hand pressure-point usage.

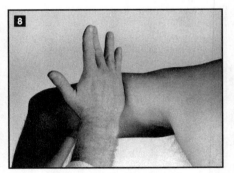

Proper position of knife-edge hand to execute roll.

Apply rolling pressure to radial nerve...

...and bring the attacker down...

...to the ground, dropping to your right knee.

Place your right knee on the upper part of his forearm—just below the elbow at point 78 or 79 (radial nerve) for submission. Shift weight slowly onto your right knee, as the submission can become painful. (**Option:** *On the street, drop down on point 79 with your kneecap.*)

Technique 11: Arm Pull Throw

(Ude Hiki Nage)

Submission: Wrist-Lock Press (Tekubi Shimi Waza)
Attack: Lapel Grab
Pressure Points: 58, 59

Ready position.

Attacker grabs your lapel.

Break his grip by reaching over his hand and grabbing it with your fingers as your thumb presses down on point 58 (between his thumb and index finger).

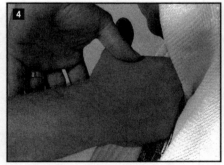

Proper placement of your thumb on attacker's hand at point 58.

Technique 13:
Body Striking Technique
(Atemi Waza)

Submission:	Finger Brace Rear Arm-Block Submission (Yubi Shimi Waza)
Attack:	Hit
Pressure Points:	36, 68

Ready position.

Attacker hits with his right fist. You block with your left forearm.

Step in with your right foot as your right hand comes across your body to...

...strike attacker with a backhand or knife-edge strike at the side base of his ribs at point 36 (floating ribs).

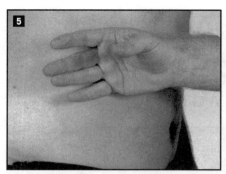

Positioning for backhand. (*Caution: A swift backhand can crack these ribs.*)

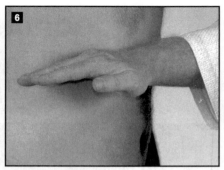

Positioning for knife-edge strike.

Your right hand cups under the attacker's right elbow and your right thumb presses on point 68 (ulnar nerve), lifting it as your left hand grabs his forearm at the wrist.

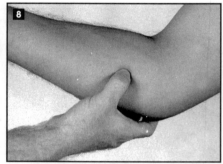

Your right thumb presses at point 68 to cause sufficient pain/distraction so you can bend his arm at the elbow.

Pull his elbow toward you as you rotate your left hand so your thumb is up and...

...push his arm behind him and up into a simple arm-lock.

Bend attacker's hand further toward him as you start to turn it to your left.

Hook his bent elbow with your cupped right hand (middle finger in his elbow joint) and pull it to you as you pivot your left foot back...

...to bring him down. (***Note:*** *In practice, use caution when bringing the attacker down.)*

After he goes down, rotate your right hand counterclockwise so it rests on the backside of his elbow. Place the back of his hand on the ground and press down on his upper arm (just above the elbow) to execute wrist-press submission.

Technique 14 (variation): Elbow Lift Rear Throw

(Hiji Ushiro Nage)

Submission:	Elbow-Joint Wind (Heji No Maki)
Attack:	Hit
Pressure Points:	60, 61

Note: *Although this has the same Japanese description as "elbow rear throw," it is a different technique. Professor Seki used a lot of generic names to describe different techniques. I've done my best to differentiate between them in this context for learning ease. –G.K.*

Ready position.

Attacker swings. Deflect the strike to your right using a circular block with your right forearm.

Your left hand comes up and grabs his hand from behind, with your thumb resting on point 60 (digital nerve) or 61 (ulnar nerve).

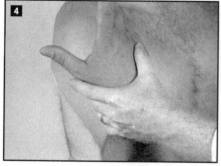

Press point 60 or 61 and immediately bend his hand toward him.

Bend his hand further toward him as you start to turn it to your left.

Cup his elbow in your right hand and pull it to you as you pivot your left foot back and...

...rotate your hand counterclockwise so that his hand is in your hand and bent inward at the wrist.

Continue to bring his elbow up. *(**Note:** Your right fingers are pointing up as you've rotated your hand.)*

Continue to move his elbow up counterclockwise as you bring his wrist down counterclockwise, pivoting your left foot back at the same time to bring him down.

Keep your left hand on his elbow and pull up quickly on his wrist for submission. *(**Caution:** **DO NOT** use this wrist maneuver in practice. Let go of wrist in practice of submission. Completing it will cause very severe joint damage, especially to the elbow.)*

105

Technique 15:
Winding Arm Throw
(Ude No Makikomi)

Submission:	Knife Submission (Katana Tatake)
Attack:	Knife thrust
Pressure Points:	45, 60

Ready position.

Attacker thrusts knife. Move your body out of the way by pivoting your right foot back in a clockwise circle.

Grab his right hand with your right hand. Rest your middle finger on point 60 (on the back of his hand between second and third fingers) and your last two fingers wrapped around the base of his hand.

Your left hand comes up and presses at point 45 (supraclavicular nerve) about one-third of the way from his neck to his shoulder.

106

Note proper position. Middle finger presses point 45 as index finger adds support/pressure.

Immediately after pressing point 45, bring his knife hand up to the left side of his neck and...

...pivot your left foot back to bring him down in a controlled manner...

...so that his knife is against his neck and your left middle finger is still pressing at point 45.

To complete the formal kata, pull the knife back across the side of his neck. (**Note:** *This is for demonstrating a complete kata. Cutting a person's neck in a street situation will probably be considered excessive force and put YOU in jail!*)

Technique 16:
Forward Winding Throw
(Mae Makikomi)

Submission: Wrist-Press Arm Pin (Tekubi (Ude) Shimi Waza)
Attack: Knife thrust
Pressure Points: 60, 75

Ready position.

Pivot your right foot back clockwise to move your body out of the way and avoid the knife thrust.

Your left hand grabs his right hand from behind; rest your thumb on point 60 (below knuckles, between second and third fingers).

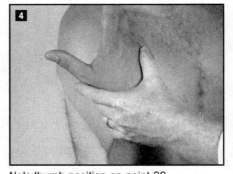

Note thumb position on point 60.

Step your left foot over his head to his left shoulder. Start to slide your right foot in a clockwise direction as you...

...go down, sliding your right leg under his head. His head should be tight against your crotch. This will be easy to do if you keep the armbar set. A properly set armbar may also apply pressure to points 77 and 78 (radial nerve), at or just above the elbow.

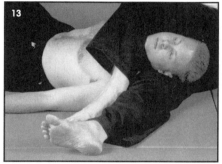

Note that your left foot is to the right of your right leg at this point.

Your left foot moves over to the left of your right leg and hooks tightly under attacker's chin.

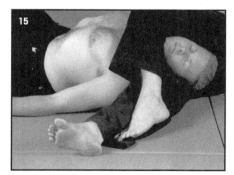

Your left foot hooks under your right calf. Roll your body slightly to your left to hyperextend attacker's neck, thus applying pressure to point 23 (center of neck) and causing his head to move back.
(Caution: Perform this move carefully!)

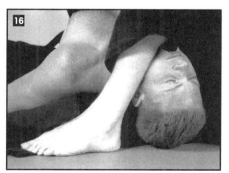

Keep your left calf as tight as possible against the left side of the attacker's neck to possibly affect points 17 and 18 while increasing effectiveness of the neck scissor.

113

Technique 18: Neck Side Throw
(Kubi Shimi Yoko Nage)

Submission: Neck Scissor Submission (Kubi Shioku Waza)
Attack: Wrist Grab (Left to Right)
Pressure Points: 14, 17

Ready position; attacker grabs your right wrist.

Turn to your right as you bring your right hand up along his stomach and toward his face in a clockwise circle.

Bring your right hand around the back of his neck to point 14 (occipital nerve) on the right side.

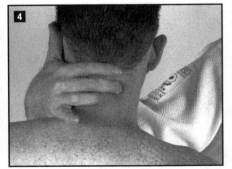

Note placement of middle finger, which is supported by other fingers at point 14. Press the tip of your middle finger at this location.

Pressing the nerve will cause attacker to turn inward (counterclockwise from your perspective) toward you.

Continue pressure on the nerve as you pivot your left foot back so you can...

...bring him down to the ground. Be sure to go down onto your right knee.

Continue pressure on the occipital nerve to pull him up so the back of his head is resting on your left thigh.

Your left hand clamps onto your right wrist (with your left forearm against the right side of attacker's neck), setting a scissor-like clamp along the left and right sides of his neck. Note that your left foot also steps to the inside of his left arm as shown and pulls back so attacker can't rest on his left elbow.

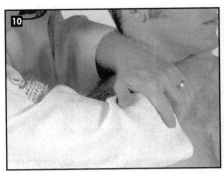 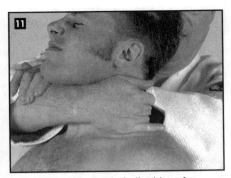

Opposite views of neck-clamping technique, which applies pressure to both sides of attacker's neck at point 17.

 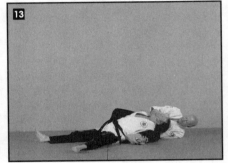

Fall back, trapping his left forearm with your left foot.

Your right leg comes up over his right upper arm (as shown). If possible, slide your right foot under the lower right section of his back.

Finish submission by straightening out and pressing point 14 in the back of his neck. Your body should be turned 30 degrees to 45 degrees from the vertical axis of his body.

...to **carefully** set the armbar. If you were tight against your attacker when you had him on his side and initiated the armbar, his shoulder should be in your crotch as you complete it.

Technique 20: Head Throw

(Atama Nage)

Submission: (Included in technique.)
Attack: Front Choke
Pressure Points: 17, 19, 26

Ready position.

Attacker sets choke.

Both of your hands come up underneath and inside his arms.

Your hands rest on his shoulders as your thumbs...

...press down and toward his back in a kneading fashion on points 26 (auricular nerves), releasing the attacker's choke and forcing his head forward.

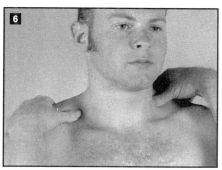

Proper placement of cupped hands on attacker's shoulders.

After his head comes forward, bring your hands up and cup them quickly (slapping them) against both sides of his neck at the base of his head, impacting points 17 and 19.

Proper placement of cupped hands.

Turn attacker's head to your right as you pivot your left foot back in a counterclockwise circle...

...to bring him down.

Once he's down…

…quickly turn his head in the other direction (toward you) to complete the kata. *(**Note:** Use **caution** as you turn the attacker's head toward you to avoid injuring him.)*

Technique 21:
Nerve Attack Takedown
(Ude Shioku Waza)

Submission: Wrist Nerve Attack (Tekubi Shioku Waza)
Attack: Lapel Grab
Pressure Points: 66, 69

Ready position.

Attacker grabs your lapel.

Your right hand comes up, reaches over his right hand and...

...executes a one-eighth to one-quarter clockwise turn so the outside of his forearm is facing upward and his elbow is facing outward.

Your left hand comes up on the outside of his right arm and rests gently on his forearm as your right finger presses down on point 69 (radial nerve).

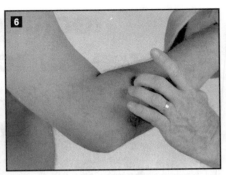

Location of point 69 (radial nerve). Note how defender's right hand is keeping attacker's right wrist bent.

Continue applying pressure down and toward you to bring attacker down, keeping his right hand against you.

Grip on attacker's right wrist, which will change as he heads toward the ground.

Once he is down, make sure your grip on his hand has changed accordingly (see detail in photo 10) as you turn your hands down (thumbs away) in a circular motion while exerting pressure at point 66 (dorsal branch of ulnar nerve) on the outside base of his right hand with the third finger of your right hand. This will hyperextend his inner wrist (below his thumb).

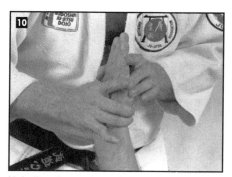

Note the change in your grip on the
attacker's right wrist as he goes down.

Technique 22: Alternate Submission for Technique 21

Submission: Wrist Bicep Press (Tekubi Shimi Waza)
Pressure Points: 75

Once the attacker is down...

...rotate his hand counterclockwise so that...

...his fingers are pointed in the same direction as his head.

Grip on attacker's right hand.

Step over his right arm and...

 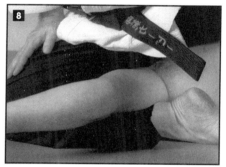

...slide your calf under his arm as you go down onto your right knee.

If properly placed, this should put pressure on point 75 (ulnar nerve) as your body weight shifts to your right side during the submission.

Shift your weight to your right leg and press down on the back of his wrist (his elbow is on the ground) to execute wrist-press submission. (*Caution: It's possible to break his wrist using this technique.*)

Technique 23:
Post-Technique-21
Submission Variation

Submission: Neck Nerve Attack (Kubi Shimi Waza)
Attack: Submission From Rear
Pressure Points: 15

Initial position.

Attacker starts to get up. You step forward, place your hands on the side of his neck and slide up, bending your middle fingers so they hook up into jawbone.

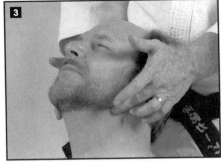

Proper placement of hands/fingers on each side of attacker's neck into point 15 (mastoid nerve and others).

Pull him back and...

Once the attacker is above your head...

Alternate view of attacker's position relative to yours.

...roll in toward him as your right arm goes around his neck.

Alternate view of right-arm maneuver against attacker.

Once the reverse head lock is set, either lean back **carefully** (thus applying pressure to point 23 [rear center of neck at second vertebra] with your forearm) **OR**...

Alternate view of backward lean.

...bring your head down against his chest to set reverse head-lock submission.

Alternate view of head placement on attacker's chest.

Technique 26:
Nerve Attack Hip Throw
(Shioku Koshi Nage)

Submission: (Included in technique.)
Attack: Front Bear Hug Under Arms
Pressure Points: 51

Ready position.

Attacker sets front bear hug.

Grab skin slightly to the rear of attacker's sides, just above his waistline at point 51 (lateral cutaneus).

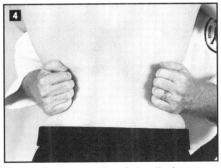

Proper placement of hands to attack nerves at point 51.

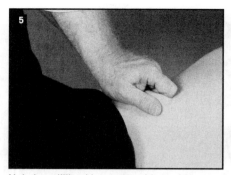

Note how little skin you need to grab!

Turn both hands inward (knuckles toward his spine) to create pain and get attacker up on his toes.

Pivot counterclockwise and...

...execute hip throw, keeping hold of the left side of his body with your left hand at point 51 as you complete the throw.

As your right knee contacts the ground, the knife-edge backhand also strikes the attacker at the base of his ribs, causing him to bend further.

Your right hand immediately comes up and executes a knife-edge strike to point 68 (ulnar nerve).

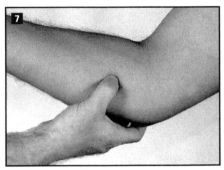

The thumb indicates where imact of knife-edge strike should occur.

The strike, combined with the pull of your left hand...

...should bring the attacker down.

Once he is down, your right hand grabs his sleeve and pulls it to your right as...

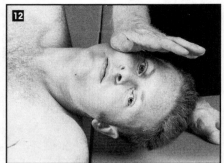

...your left hand lets go and executes an open-palm strike to his right cheekbone at point 9.

Close-up of proper open-palm strike. Contact with cheekbone at point 9 is made with the base of the palm.

Technique 29:
Shoulder Nerve-Attack Takedown

(Senaka Shioku Waza)

Submission:	None
Attack:	Front Choke
Pressure Points:	46

Ready position.

Attacker sets front choke.

Both of your hands come up from inside and...

...rest on his shoulders.

Dig in at point 46 (lateral nerve) with left-hand fingers (if left foot is forward), causing attacker's right shoulder to go down to avoid pain.

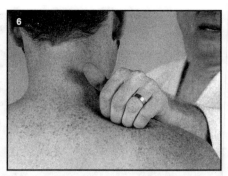

Note proper position of hands and fingers. Dig in by rolling xxxbehind and under the horizontal notch of the trapezius muscle in his shoulder. Maintain pressure throughout technique.

Pivot your left foot back...

...bringing attacker down.

Retreat into ready position.

Continue to press on point 75 as you pull his arm toward you with your right hand. Simulatneously push his right forearm away with your left arm...

...as you pivot your left foot back, causing the attacker to go down.

Once the attacker is down, bend his wrist so the back of his hand is facing the mat.

Place the back of his hand against the mat and press down on his upper arm to set wrist press.

Technique 32: Cross-Choke Winding Throw
(Maki No Shioku Waza)

Submission: (Included in technique.)
Attack: Single- or Double-Lapel Grab
Pressure Points: 17, 19, 21

Ready position.

Attacker grabs your lapel(s).

As attacker pulls you into him, your right hand grabs high on his right lapel and your left hand grabs his left lapel at mid-chest level.

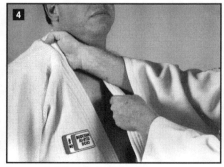

Proper clothing grab. Pull with your left hand, which will cause your right forearm to go up into point 17, 19 and 21 as a choke is set.

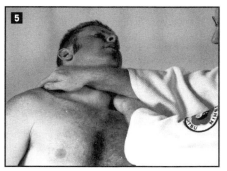

No shirt? No problem. Grab over attacker's shoulders at the base of his neck. Pull with your left hand.

A more open view of cross-choke being set.

Pivot your right foot back...

...as you bring the attacker...

...down to the ground...

...and go down onto your right knee.

Submit by pulling up on attacker's left lapel or, if he's not wearing a shirt, pull up on his left shoulder as you press down with your right forearm and simultaneously pull it to your right.

Push the attacker's forearm back as you maintain position of his upper arm to initiate takedown.

Pivot your left foot back as he goes down.

Once attacker is down, step around his head with left foot, turning his arm clockwise...

...to get him onto his stomach. Make sure your knees are against him.

Squat down on the attacker, bringing his arm into a lock.

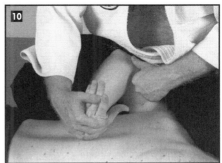

Arm lock set with wrist-press.

If the attacker is facing you, use verbal commands (and either wrist-press or nerve-press) to get him to face away from you. This actually makes submission more effective.

If attacker becomes uncooperative, shift your weight so that your right knee presses down on the side of his neck (base of head) to secure compliance.

Technique 35:
Side Wrist-Lock Takedown
(Tekubi Shioku Waza)

Submission: None
Attack: Lapel Grab
Pressure Points: 67, 70

Ready position.

Attacker grabs your left lapel.

Both of your hands come up across his wrist, right over left, facing you.

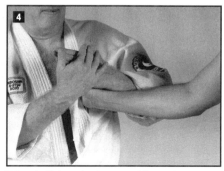

Bring both hands down and toward your chest, keeping hands in place against it.

Turn your body clockwise to get attacker off balance.

Note how your left forearm presses down on his lower forearm at point 67 (halfway down the forearm at the base of the brachoradialis) as you turn your body to your left.

(**Note:** *Don't bend over or you'll lose hold.*)

Alternative: Grab left-over-right and have your right hand hook around his hand, turning it perpendicular to the ground and...

...applying pressure to point 70 (one-third of the way down from the elbow) on his right forearm as you turn to your right.

Continue downward pressure as you roll your forearm slightly forward to bring the attacker to the ground.

Once the attacker is down...

...bring his hand palm-down onto the ground and bend his fingers back.

Technique 37:
Wrist Pressure Point
(Kubi Shioku Waza)

Submission:	None
Attack:	Handshake
Pressure Points:	63

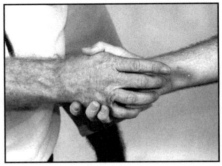

Another way to neutralize a handshake is to relax your hand. Your middle fingertip presses point 63 (on the wrist at the base of the ulnar nerve) at a 90-degree angle. Use just enough pressure to keep it there. This procedure redirects all of the attacker's ki back into his hand, neutralizing any pressure on your hand (as long as you keep your hand relaxed).

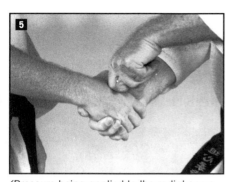

(Pressure being applied to the radial nerve at point 58.)

...and bring the attacker down to the ground.

Technique 40:
Winding Strike Attack
(Makikomi Shioku Waza)

Submission: Knee-Drop Submission (Ashi-Ate)
Attack: Overhead Club
Pressure Points: 46, 76, 79

Ready position.

Attacker swings with overhead club.

Block attacker's arm outward.

Your right hand comes up and rests on his right shoulder as your left arm continues to block his right arm, sliding down toward his wrist to hook his wrist with a "C-grip" (thumb underneath and fingers on top of his wrist).

Your right fingers dig into the nerve behind his shoulder to shift his balance back as you step in with your right foot.

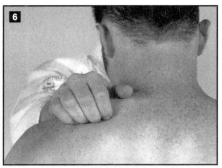

Hand placement for getting under the horizontal notch in the trapezius muscle to access point 46 (lateral nerve). Note position of right thumb.

Bring attacker down to the ground...

...while maintaining pressure on point 46.

Once the attacker is down, bring your right hand up behind his right forearm.

View of forearm position **from other side**.

169

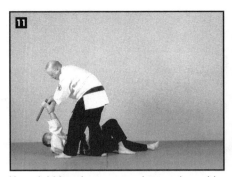

Your right hand secures a strong grip on his right wrist as your left hand lets go.

Your left hand slides to just above his elbow joint so that his upper arm (just above the elbow) is between your thumb and index finger.

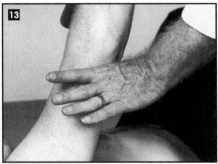

Your left hand, holding his upper arm between your thumb and index finger, is almost at a right angle to his elbow. Pressure is applied to point 76 (ulnar nerve; just above the thumb joint) with the inside ridge of your hand.

Roll attacker's elbow in a clockwise direction as you pivot your right foot back, bringing attacker up into a temporary sitting position.

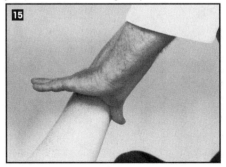

Close-up of positioning for clockwise turn.

Continue clockwise turn until attacker is rotated onto his stomach for final submission. (**Note:** *Left hand is still applying pressure to keep attacker down.*)

Place/drop your left knee on attacker's arm just above your left hand. In practice, shift your weight slowly to your left kneecap to secure submission as you apply pressure to point 79 (radial nerve).

Technique 41:
Elbow Attack Side Throw
(Hiji Tatake Yoko Nage)

Submission:	Shoulder Pin (Ude Gatame)
Attack:	Lapel Grab
Pressure Points:	25, 68, 69

Ready position.

Attacker grabs your left lapel. Your left hand comes out and up in clockwise direction...

...so that the outer edge of your hand...

...comes down, resting on his right forearm at point 69 (about one-third of the way down from his elbow).

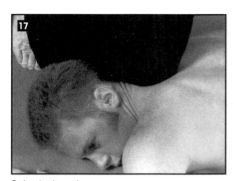

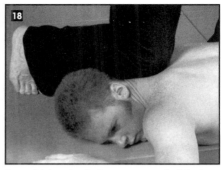

Submission close-up.

For safety's sake, balance on your foot (note position of toes) and kneecap to reduce and more effectively control the amount of pressure applied via kneecap-press to point 25.

Technique 42:
Neck Attack
(Kubi Tatake)

Submission:	Reverse Pin/Wrist-Press Lift (Ude Gatame)
Attack:	Head Lock Pin on Ground
Pressure Points:	14

You're in a head lock with your right arm pinned. *(**Note:** This counter will work **ONLY** if this hold is not completely set.)*

Shift your hips so your weight is on your right "cheek." Your right upper arm lodges just below attacker's skull. Form a right fist and bend your right forearm parallel to the ground. Grab fist with your left hand.

Quickly push/jerk your right forearm against the base of his skull/back of his neck at point 14 (occipital nerve), turning your body to the right immediately thereafter.

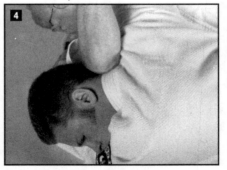

Position of right upper arm against attacker's neck.

Press the tip of the attacker's thumbnail at point 56 at a 45-degree angle until he lets go of the handshake and you can slide your hand out.

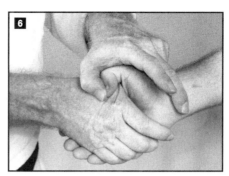

Apply pressure to the thumb-tip very slowly, as it can be quite painful.

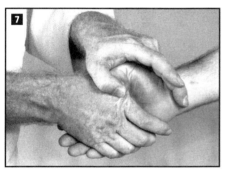

Note that the attacker's thumb is being pushed **down** toward the base of his thumb, **NOT** up and over his wrist.

Once you have removed your right hand, maintain pressure on his thumb. Move his hand up in a counterclockwise direction...

...as you pivot your left foot back...

...to throw the attacker. Be sure to maintain pressure on the thumb for pain and control purposes.

Once he is on the ground...

...you can use the thumb-tip press for submission. You can also bring him back up into a standing position or roll him over onto his stomach using appropriate thumb-tip pressure.

Technique 45:
Forward Finger Throw
(Mae Yubi Nage)

Submission: Finger Bend (Yubi Shimi Waza)
Attack: Rear Mugging (Arm-Lock and Hand Over Mouth)
Pressure Points: 84, 85

Attacker sets mugging hold (right hand over your mouth and your left arm in an arm lock).

Your left foot comes up and...

...its heel strikes down on the instep of the attacker's left foot, striking point 84 (dorsal or plantar nerve) or 85 (plantar nerve).

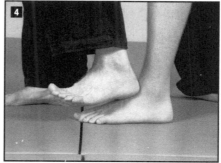

This part of the foot is generally unprotected, regardless of the footwear worn by an attacker. Even your bare foot is effective here.

Bring your left arm out of the arm lock.

The attacker is still holding on to your forearm, so bring his arm up as you sidestep and go under his arm (which should be twisted so his palm ends up facing sideways or upward).

Your right hand grabs his hand from the backside and turns it palm-up.

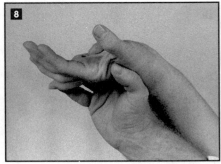

Note how attacker's hand is gripped, as well as how his wrist is twisted clockwise by this point. You are now set up to execute a wrist-twist forward finger throw.

Move into your forward throw by keeping his wrist twisted and hand bent back for control purposes.

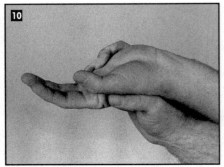

Note how your hand and forearm are in a straight line under his forearm. This creates additional leverage and control for the throw.

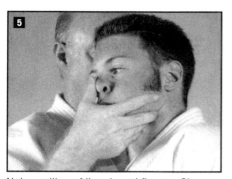

Note position of thumb and fingers. Close your hand, bringing thumb and middle finger together as much as possible for maximum pressure on the infraorbital and vagus nerves.

Turn attacker's face to your right as your left arm reaches out.

Your left hand hooks on to attacker's right arm (just above his bent elbow) and pushes his arm to your right.

This will turn the attacker around so his back is toward you. Maintain pressure on nerves with your right thumb and middle finger.

Your left hand lets go of attacker's right upper arm and comes around to his left side.

Reach through his bent left arm on the inside and...

...grab onto his left forearm from on top. Your thumb should also be on top.

Pull his arm back into an arm lock.
*(**Note:** This is actually an improper arm lock.)*

Set arm lock as high as possible, maintaining pressure on attacker's nose. Step back so attacker is off balance (as indicated by his arched back).

Technique 47:
Shoulder Attack
Circle Throw
(Senaka Guruma)

Submission:	Cross-Choke Head Pin (Atama Gatame)
Attack:	Double Hit
Pressure Points:	21, 45

Ready position.

Attacker hits with his right; block it out and away from you.

As attacker swings with his left, step in with your right foot and block his left hit out and away from you.

Once both of his arms are blocked outward…

...bring both of your hands (palms down) downward—one on each side of his head. Do not go above his head.

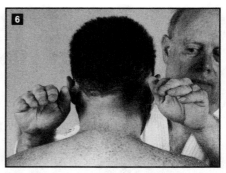

With attacker's head squarely between your hands, you have other options should you be unable to continue with technique. *(Author's note: I prefer to get to ear level before starting downward strike.)*

Quickly strike downward onto his shoulders at point 45 with both hands open.

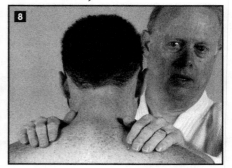

Note strike zone on his shoulders. The impact from this should disorient the attacker and destroy his kuzushi.

Immediately after impact, your fingers should part slightly and press at point 45 (into the lateral nerves), thus causing attacker to bend forward. *(Author's note: I always do this because you should never asume a technique will work. You should always have two or three options at your disposal.)*

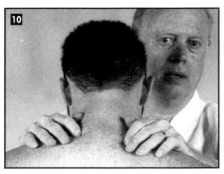

Note how fingers are slightly apart, making it easier to get to the nerves in the shoulder.

Release nerves as you grab clothing on his shoulders and "steer" him to your left while...

...pivoting your left foot back, thus throwing the attacker...

...to the ground.

Once the attacker is on the ground, go down onto your right knee. Bring your right forearm across, under his chin.

Bring your left forearm down under his chin, between your right forearm and his chin. Both of your forearms should be under his chin with palms up. Keep hold of his gi.

191

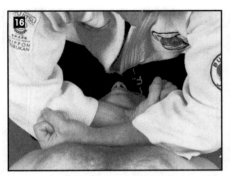

Note position of both forearms. By keeping the forearms in an upward position as you finish submission, you maximize backward movement of his head and can place additional pressure on point 21 (larynx) as well as the nerves at the base of his jawbone. *(**Note:** Use **caution** as you set this hold **slowly** and for the rest of the submission.)*

Lie down with your chest on attacker's face to finish submission.

...strike down at his elbow as you turn your body to your right.

Your left hand (middle finger straight with other fingers supporting it) then presses into his throat at point 22 (jugular notch).

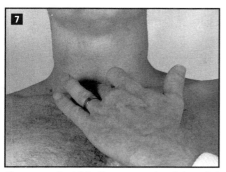

Close-up of middle finger pressing into point 22. (**Note:** *In practice, press* **slowly***.*)

Press straight toward the back of his neck as you pivot your right leg back to complete the throw.

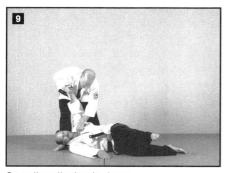

Once the attacker is down...

...step over him with your left foot. Lean attacker forward as you do this so he is slightly beyond being on his right side. (**Note:** *Leaning attacker forward this much will allow for a much tighter and more secure armbar submission.*)

Bring your right foot over his head as you immediately begin to squat down to set up armbar pin.

Roll onto your back, thus setting armbar and pin.

In top view of roll-back, note how attacker's shoulder is tight against your crotch. If you lean the attacker's body slightly forward before going into an armbar (or similar hold), it will **always** result in a very tight hold, lock or pin.

Depending on your leg length, you may also slip the instep of your right foot under the attacker's shoulder. If your calf is also resting across the attacker's throat at the same time, it creates a leverage situation in which the attacker fights against himself if he tries to lift his head.

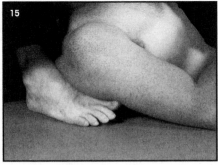

Note how your foot should be turned so it is under the attacker's shoulder.

Technique 50: Nerve Attack Winding Throw

(Shioku Waza)

Submission: Wrist-Lock Life Neck Scissors (Tekubi Gatame)
Attack: Hit or Club
Pressure Points: 23, 31

Ready position.

Attacker swings at you with a club.

Step forward slightly with your left foot as you block attacker's right forearm; after block, grab his wrist/forearm.

Your right arm moves up toward attacker's left armpit.

Your right fingers (straight, together and with palm facing you) strike/slide in behind his pectoral muscles at point 31 (front of the shoulder, a little below 2 o'clock) as you step forward with your right leg.

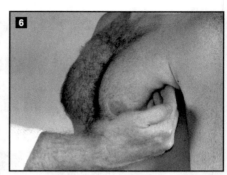

Note position of right fingers and hand, which is moving in a counterclockwise direction as you move your body in a counterclockwise circle.

Pivot your left foot back to throw the attacker, keeping hold of his left wrist.

Attacker is thrown to the ground.

You should still have hold of attacker's right sleeve/wrist after he's down.

Start to set up wrist-lock lift submission by bringing your right arm inside his right arm.

Technique 52:
Knee-Drop Neck Throw
(Kubi Otoshi)

Submission: Neck Nerve Scissors (Kubi Tatake)
Attack: Front Choke
Pressure Points: 14, 17, 18, 35

Ready position.

Attacker chokes you.

Your left hand grabs high on attacker's left sleeve from the outside. Right hand is ready to strike his solar plexus.

Strike point 35 (solar plexus) as a distraction move. It should break the attacker's kuzushi and cause him to lean forward slightly. (**Note:** *If it's not effective, that's OK. The forward lean is not essential to complete the technique.*)

Your right hand comes up in a cupped position below his ear (about 4 to 8 inches away from his neck).

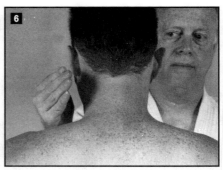

Note position of cupped hand parallel to the attacker's neck.

Cupped hand strikes attacker's neck (just below his ear), thus unbalancing him by causing middle ear to de-equilibrate momentarily. If done properly, you will hear a "pop" rather than a "slap" and your partner shouldn't feel anything (as opposed to a slap).

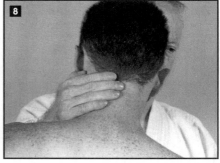

Note position of cupped hand at impact. (**Note:** *In practice, keep your fingers slightly apart as you strike in case your partner lowers his head and you strike his ear instead. This will help protect his ear from injury.*)

Pull attacker counterclockwise as you pivot in to execute a *tai otoshi* (drop throw).

Execute the drop throw, keeping your right hand in place at the side of his neck.

As attacker goes down, drop onto your right knee.

Press at point 14 (occipital nerve) with your right middle finger to raise attacker's head. Clamp your left hand onto your right forearm as close to your wrist as possible.

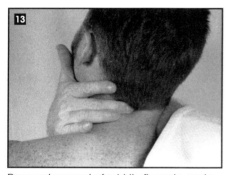

Proper placement of middle finger to apply pressure to occipital nerve.

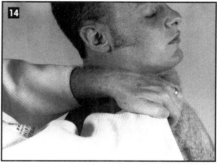

Note how left hand clamps onto right forearm from its top side. Your right hand/forearm should be as close as possible to the right side of the attacker's neck so that pressure can be applied to points 17 (under the jaw) and 18 (halfway down the side of the neck, at the front of the sternocleidomastoid muscle) via "scissor effect" (achieved by pulling up with your right hand as your left forearm presses down against the right side of the attacker's neck).

Make sure attacker's head is on your left thigh. Set submission as described in photo 14.

Technique 53:
One-Arm Drop-Throw
(Ippon Otoshi)

Submission: Winding Armbar (Ude Guruma)
Attack: Low Rear Bear Hug
Pressure Points: 99

Ready position.

Attacker sets bear hug from behind.

Your right thumb presses at point 99 (tibial nerve) on the inside of his right thigh to secure release or relaxation of the bear hug.

Correct location of pressure point for this portion of the technique.

...down to the ground.

Technique 55:
Neck Nerve Press
(Kubi Shioku Waza)

Submission: None
Attack: Sleeve Grab (Left to Right Wrist)
Pressure Points: 26

Ready position.

Attacker grabs your right sleeve or wrist.

Bring your open right hand under his forearm and out to your right in a counterclockwise motion.

Continue the counterclockwise circle (which will lock his wrist) and reach toward his chest. Then move up to his neck so you can press point 26 (auricular nerve) as you step forward with your right foot.

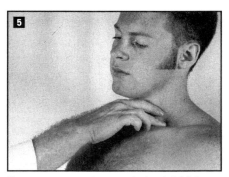

Proper pressure placement at point 26 to continue technique.

Straighten out your right arm, pressing point 26 (auricular nerve)...

...thus causing the attacker to fall backward.

Technique 56:
Forearm Nerve Attack
(Ude Shioku Waza)

Submission: Knee Face-Press (Kao Shioku Waza)
Attack: Lapel Grab and Pull
Pressure Points: 8, 67

Ready position.

Attacker grabs your lapel.

As he pulls you toward him, place your left hand on his upper forearm below the elbow.

Step in with your right foot as he pulls you. At the same time, press point 67 (cutaneus, radial nerves) in his upper forearm, making sure the underside of his forearm is against your chest.

Balance Point 3

Pressure Point Used: 39

 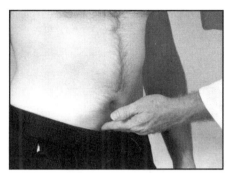

Location: Two to three inches below navel. Press inward and down at about a 20- to 30-degree angle with either hand, palm up.

Balance Point 4

Pressure Point Used: 41

 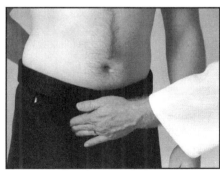

Location: Halfway down right torso-leg joint. Push inward toward rear of body with left palm racing right.

Balance Point 5

Pressure Point Used: 41

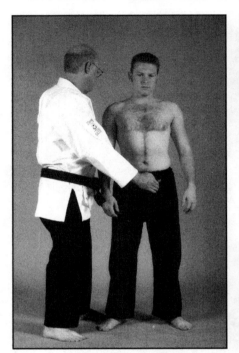 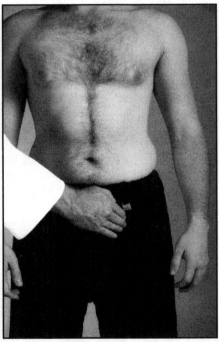

Location: Halfway down left torso-leg joint. Push inward toward rear of body with right palm facing left.

Balance Point 6

Pressure Point Used: 54

 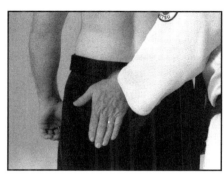

Location: Top of left buttock. Press inward at 30- to 45-degree angle with either palm (facing buttock). Push with base of palm.

Balance Point 7

Pressure Point Used: 54

 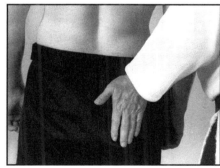

Location: Top of right buttock. Press inward at 30- to 45-degree angle with either palm (facing buttock). Push with base of palm.

Balance Point 8

Pressure Point Used: 95

Location: Behind left knee joint. Quick strike inward with inside of right foot (if you're on his left side) or inside of left foot (if you're on his right side).

Balance Point 9

Pressure Point Used: 95

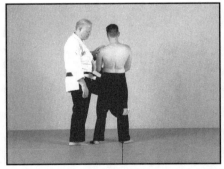 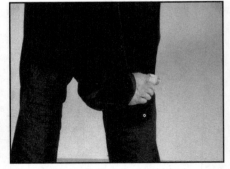

Location: Behind right knee joint. Quick strike inward with inside of right foot (if you're on his left side) or inside of left foot (if you're on his right side).

CHAPTER 9

BALANCE-POINT TECHNIQUES

Balance-Point Technique 1: Upper Torso Right Turnaround

Pressure Point Used: 32

Ready position.

Gently place your left hand on opponent's right upper arm. If you grab him, he will definitely pull away from you.

Gently place your right middle finger on balance point 2.

Push balance point 2 with your right middle finger and pull his right shoulder to you with your left hand, turning opponent around.

View of push and torso turn from reverse angle.

Opponent should end up with his shoulders against your upper chest. There are a number of techniques you can do from this point to control him if necessary.

View of completed turnaround from reverse angle.

Balance-Point Technique 2: Forward Bend Over Straight

Pressure Point Used: 39

Your right hand rests on opponent's left shoulder.

Your left hand (palm up, middle finger extended with other fingers supporting) rests 2 to 3 inches below his saiki tanden at balance point 3 (pressure point 39).

Push inward with your left fingers as your right hand guides him forward and downward.

Balance-Point Technique 3: Forward Right Bend Over

Pressure Point Used: 41

Your right hand rests on opponent's left shoulder. Place your left fingers on balance point 4 (pressure point 41).

Push in with your left fingers to get opponent to bend to his right. Your right hand pulls his left shoulder toward you at the same time.

Balance-Point Technique 4: Forward Left Bend Over

Pressure Point Used: 41

Your left hand rests on opponent's right shoulder.

Place your right middle finger (with other fingers supporting) on balance point 5 (pressure point 41).

Push in at balance point 5 to get opponent to bend to his left (your right). (***Note:*** *Pulling him slightly with your left hand to "assist" in the turn is often helpful.*)

Balance-Point Technique 5: Back Arch (Left Side)

Pressure Point Used: 54

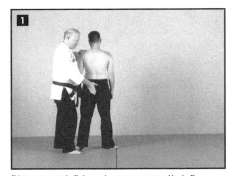

Place your left hand on opponent's left shoulder.

Placing right hand on balance point 6 (left buttock), push on point 54 (sciatic nerve) as you guide his shoulders back with your left hand.

Balance-Point Technique 6: Back Arch (Right Side)

Pressure Point Used: 55

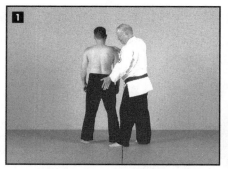

Place your right hand on opponent's right shoulder.

Placing your left hand on opponent's buttocks, push on point 55 (center base of back) as you guide his shoulders back with your right hand.

Balance-Point Technique 7: Left Knee Joint Off Balance

Pressure Point Used: 95

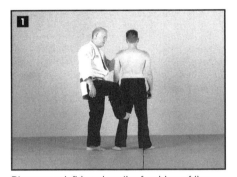

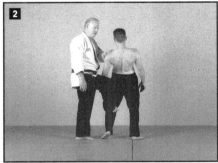

Place your left hand on the front top of the opponent's left shoulder. Give a quick tap behind his left knee joint (balance point 8/ pressure point 95) with you r right foot and...

...guide him down with your left hand. Be sure to move your right foot out of the way when he falls.

Glossary

aikido: joint locks and using attacker's ki or momentum

atemi waza: attacking vital areas

budo: spiritual rather than combative approach to martial arts

dan: degree of black belt rank

do: way(s)

dojo: training hall

gi: uniform

gingitzu: clenched fist with middle knuckle extended slightly

hanshi: master

ikkyu: first-degree brown belt

ippon otoshi: one-arm drop-throw

ippon seoi nage: one-arm hip-throw

judan: 10th-degree black belt

judo: throws and pins

juji: cross-block

jujitsu: "gentle art"

karatedo: hits and kicks

kata: specific form or technique

ki: energy flow

koshi nage: hip throw

kuzushi: balance

kyu: level below black belt

maitta: "I quit!" or "I give up!"

mushin: empty/clear mind which is open and unfixed yet ready for response without conscious thought

nidan: second-degree black belt

obi: belt

ryu: styles

saiki tanden: lower stomach

sandan: third-degree black belt

sankyu: three steps below first-degree black belt

sensei: teacher

shioku waza: pain and/or nerve techniques

shodan: first-degree black belt

shuto: edge of the hand

tachi waza: standing ready position

tai otoshi: drop throw

te nage: hand throw

tori: person executing a technique

ude guruma: shoulder lock

uke: partner

waza: complete technique

yonkyu: four degrees below black belt

yudansha: individual with a black belt

Recommended Reading

Alexander, George and Ken Penland. *Bubishi: The Martial Spirit*. Lake Worth, FL: Yamazato Publications, 1993.

Cerney, J.V. *Acupuncture Without Needles*. West Nyack, NY: Parker Publishing Co., 1974.

Daniels, Lucille, M.A., and Catherine Worthingham, Ph.D. *Muscle Testing: Techniques of Examination*. Philadelphia: W.B. Saunders Co., 1972.

Goch, Michael R. *Acupressure's Potent Points*. New York: Bantam Books, 1990.

Gray, Henry. *Gray's Anatomy*. Orlando: House of Collectibles, Inc., 1934.

Kirby, George. *Jujitsu: Basic Techniques of the Gentle Art*. Santa Clarita, CA: Ohara Publications Inc., 1983.

Kirby, George. *Jujitsu: Intermediate Techniques of the Gentle Art*. Santa Clarita, CA: Ohara Publications Inc., 1985.

Naisbitt, John. *Megatrends: 10 New Directions Transforming Our Lives*. New York: Warner Books, 1982.

Namikoshi, Tokujiro. *Shiatsu*. Tokyo: Japan Publications Inc., 1969.

Seriwaza, Katsusuke, M.D. *Tsubo: Vital Points for Oriental Therapy*. Tokyo: Japan Publications Inc., 1976.

Travel, Janet G., M.D., and David G. Simons, M.D. *Myofascial Pain and Dysfunction: The Trigger Point Manual*. Baltimore: Lippincott, Williams & Wilkins, 1983.

Additionally, excellent reference charts on the nervous system, human musculature and trigger points can be obtained by contacting the Anatomical Chart Co. in Skokie, Illinois, at (800) 621-7500 or visiting their Web site at www.anatomical.com.

Other Books by George Kirby

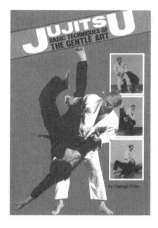

JUJITSU:
Basic Techniques of the Gentle Art
In his classic 1983 text, American Jujitsu Association (AJA) co-founder and award-winning instructor George Kirby presents the "gentle art" of *jujitsu*. Fully illustrated with sequenced photos, this easy-to-follow guide discusses *ki* (internal energy), using momentum, joint locks, throws, pressure points and nerve attacks. Includes easy-reference chart of jujitsu techniques applicable to various attack situations and scoring criteria for rank examinations. Simply a must for every jujitsu practitioner! 128 pgs.
(ISBN 0-89750-088-1) Code No. 425 – Retail $9.95

JUJITSU:
Intermediate Techniques of the Gentle Art
George Kirby returns in this acclaimed 1985 sequel with the next level in *jujitsu* training. Topics include Japanese terminology, advanced theory, defense against multiple attackers, reverses, ground defenses, staff/baton defenses and an intermediate-level technique applicability chart. Also includes testing criteria/forms for higher ranks, as well as an expanded technique index and glossary. It's the perfect complement to the AJA co-founder's first book and an obvious standard reference for every jujitsu practitioner's library! **(ISBN 0-89750-128-4) Code No. 441 – Retail $18.95**